'Derek Tangye used to work for MI5 and his wife Jeannie was Press Officer at the Savoy. What a life. Who could ask for more? They could – and they did. The Tangyes gave it all up, lock, stock and barrel, and went to live on a wild cliff in Cornwall. Their friends said they must be mad. But they knew they weren't. I know they weren't. And so will you when you read Derek Tangye's book about their life.
'A story – gentle, sad or funny – is told about all the animals and birds in their life . . . all of them are described in such fascinating detail they sound like real people'
Evening News

'Thousands of readers know the Tangyes' Cornwall cottage at Minack from his previous book that told how he and his wife got away from it all, grew daffodils and sweated and were happy with the flowers, the birds, the animals, the sea. Now this engaging writer mines another book from their experiences, such as the day the water ran out, and the day the vicar called about the oven. . . .'
Evening Standard

Cottage on a Cliff

DEREK TANGYE

SPHERE BOOKS LIMITED

A Sphere Book

First published in Great Britain in 1972 by Michael Joseph Ltd
Published by Sphere Books 1974
Reprinted 1975, 1977 (twice), 1978, 1979, 1980, 1981, 1983,
1984, 1986, 1987, 1989, 1991

ISBN 0 7221 8393 3

Printed and bound in Great Britain by
Cox & Wyman Ltd, Reading

A Division of
Macdonald & Co (Publishers) Ltd
Orbit House
1 New Fetter Lane
London EC4A 1AR
A member of Maxwell Macmillan Pergamon Publishing Corporation

To Caroline Oliver

CHAPTER ONE

Michaelmas Day is the beginning of winter. The day when retiring farmers hand over to their successors, when beefy lifeguards have departed from now deserted beaches and holiday hotels have closed till another summer, when sea-shore car parks are empty and pampered gulls wonder what has happened, when ice cream kiosks are shuttered and the winds begin to blow, when some will grumble that life has become too quiet and others will be glad the holiday season is over: 'Cornwall belongs to Cornwall again.' The visitors have gone.

There are sleepy flies on the last blackberries, spider webs stretch across narrow paths, I flush the first woodcock from a patch of battered bracken as I walk towards Carn Barges, a fieldfare in the stable meadow below the cottage looks surprised to be in a strange country, a late wasp buzzes dozily against a window of the porch, blue-tits have returned to the bird-table after being self-sufficient during the summer, faded honeysuckle still blooms in odd places down the cliff a hundred yards away, ivy leaves are yellow-green and leaves of the brambles have turned a robin-red. Wild violets are in clusters. Winter gorse is in flower.

I pull up an imaginary drawbridge at Monty's Leap when winter comes. I play a game that Jeannie and I live in a fortress with a deep moat surrounding us. We have no part in the busy, fractious, unsatisfied outside world, and nothing can disturb the easy motion of the day. Strikes, inflation, unemployment, violence, greed, envy, all these I pretend play no part in our lives. I have passing fantasies that peace of mind has been permanently obtained by looking after our own lives instead of interfering in the lives of others. I am therefore immune, I pretend, from the tedious troubles of the herd. I live in a world where time is mine. I am a countryman living in a remote place with the chance to keep my own identity. I am as simply happy as the uncomplicated peasant of a hundred years ago who never left his parish. Such a game I may play for a day, for two, for three: and then some incident will occur which wakes me up to reality.

'Ian has killed himself,' I said.

The post had arrived a few minutes before, brought by Roger on a bicycle from the village post office of St Buryan. I had opened a couple of letters, then this third one from a journalist friend in London. Jeannie was standing by the fireplace.

'I can't believe it!' And she put her hands to her face. 'Oh no. What happened? Why? Why should he have done it?'

Why, why. Always the same question. One can understand the causes of tragedy, seldom explain them.

'Read the letter,' I said, and handed it to her.

Ian was English, divorced and around forty. He had had exceptional success as a film scriptwriter; and also as co-producer of three films which have become classics. He was, and this I particularly remembered in the light of what had happened, a comfortable person to be with, an easy-going person with a wish to please, a good friend, and generous. We used to see a good deal of him in London, and he was one of those who regularly came to our Boat Race parties when we lived at Thames Cottage overlooking the finishing post at Mortlake. After we left for Cornwall our reunions necessarily became fewer. He stayed with us here at Minack once, and by that time his circumstances had begun to change. The film group with whom he worked had broken up, and he was on his own operating as a free-lance with see-saw success. Then his luck began to run out and money to be short, and pub sandwiches took the place of expensive lunches, and a bedsitter in Fulham the place of a flat off Berkeley Square. Nevertheless he remained one of those people whose success seems always to be near if only the chance came their way; and he was on the verge of such a success when he took an overdose of sleeping tablets.

What had happened was this. He had adapted a well-known novel for a film, and his shooting script had been warmly accepted by a film company. A contract had been drafted, a famous actor had agreed to play the leading role, and so six months' hard work was about to receive its reward. The actor, however, was an international star in a position to state his own terms. He was delighted to play the

8

star part, he said, but he didn't like the shooting script . . . and he demanded that a friend of his should rewrite it. The news reached Ian in a telephone call near midnight on a Saturday. On Sunday morning he was found dead.

Part of me wants to believe in the myth that we are masters of our fates. There are occasions, no doubt, when we are in command, those occasions when we make a firm decision determining the pattern of a day, a year, and for that matter the rest of our lives. In this respect we can be masters of our fates. We are powerless, however, when it comes to the multitude of incidents that even with hind-sight we know we could not have controlled. The chance meeting, coincidences, the galaxy of times when luck plays the dominant part. We are then at the mercy of fortune and William Henley's cry, 'I am master of my fate,' becomes a mocking one. Ian, for instance, could not have controlled the timing of that telephone call. If he had received it in the morning, he would have been more resilient. Might he not have been alive today?

I still marvel at the luck that brought Jeannie and me to Minack. There are legions of people who yearn to pack up their jobs, and find some patch of land where they can create their earthly Nirvana. Jeannie and I were among that number who have succeeded in turning that dream into reality, but this was not achieved simply by exercising cold reason. We needed many unexpected circumstances to be on our side.

We both, for instance, had to share the wish to leave London, for failure would have been certain had one been dragging the other; and it would have been understandable if Jeannie had hesitated about leaving the fun she had as publicity head of the Savoy, Claridges and Berkeley. There were, too, the circumstances surrounding the discovery of Minack. The name, Lamorna, captured my imagination when I was a boy, but I never paid a visit to this lovely valley until one day in London I had a sudden urge to spend a few days' holiday there. Thus it was that Jeannie and I took a walk along the track above the harbour, then through chest-high bracken above the rocks and the sea until we climbed up the cliff to the point called Carn Barges. It was then that we saw the grey cottage inland, half hidden on the edge of a wood; and we knew from that instant we were going to live there. This intuition proved to be correct, but here again an odd circumstance helped it to be so.

At the particular time when we started to negotiate for a lease, there was a squatter scare in the area. Squatters were threatening to take possession of any cottages they found empty; and Minack was empty. It was in a desolate condition, rain leaking through the roof, rat holes in the boards that covered the earthen floor; and yet obviously it would prove to be quite satisfactory for any squatters. A potential squatter group was also nearby, living in the moorland near Lamorna; and their presence caused considerable concern to the farmer who was responsible for Minack. The group was harmless and pleasant enough, living out their theory that sharing was the secret of happiness; but the farmer was apprehensive.

Hence when we came along offering to rent the cottage, we had this luck on our side. True the farmer took time to make up his mind, but he would never have decided in our favour had it not been for the presence of the squatters. We were his answer to the squatters. He didn't really want anyone in the cottage, but there was no harm in letting it to us for a few months ... We looked respectable, I was Cornish, and our presence would keep the squatters at bay. In due course the squatters would leave the area, and also, he was sure, would we ... after all the girl would be certain to return to her glittering life at the Savoy. To his credit, when he realised his judgement about us was wrong, he did

everything possible to help us; and he became a great friend.

We depended on luck, therefore, to come here. And we have needed luck also to stay. Hence we have learnt not to take any day for granted. We are on guard. I may pull up an imaginary drawbridge at Monty's Leap when winter comes and pretend that we have no part in the fractious, outside world; but I only have to have a letter to remind me that I still belong to it.

For wherever one lives and whatever one does, contentment will always be illusive. It just happens, however, that contentment is less illusive when one lives in a place which is far from the crowd.

Ian, I know, would have liked this kind of life if he had had the luck to live it.

CHAPTER TWO

'The donkeys are hooting.'

'I heard.'

The hoots came from a distance, from the meadows overlooking the sea of Mount's Bay, bordering the track which leads to the onion meadow at the boundary of Minack land.

'What's happening?' said Jeannie.

'Usual thing, I expect. Just wanting attention.'

'Fred was sounding his alarm note ... it's the poacher again.'

'Perhaps.'

Fred was born at Minack beside a rock that grows out of the ground in the big field which was called the cemetery field because cattle used to be buried there; and which is now called Fred's field. He is a splendid-looking donkey with a fine intelligent head and a coat of chocolate-brown which is thick in winter like a moorland pony. We had bought Penny, his mother, at a pub near Redruth a month before he was born ... a black donkey with sad eyes and a coat which was in a moth-eaten condition. The publican said she had no future. He explained that after her foal was born she was to be sent to the knacker's yard while the foal was scheduled to go to a travelling circus. Such talk was

11

good salesmanship. It was persuasive enough for Jeannie to say that she wouldn't leave the pub unless Penny came with us; and that was that. Penny returned with us to Minack in the back of the Land Rover.

'You had better go and see what's happening,' said Jeannie.

It was a lovely morning. A morning that belonged to summer. A still sea, soft salty scents, a quiet sky. I could have believed it was a June morning except there were no swallows dancing in the sky or darting in and out of the barn door; and the bracken swathing the moorland was a red-brown instead of a rich green, and spider webs shimmered on the hedges, and the leaves of the elms had begun to fall in the wood, and buds were plumply showing on the December-flowering camellia bush. The year was lying about its age. It had produced this Indian summer to fool the Red Admiral butterfly that fluttered from leaf to leaf on the escallonia opposite the entrance to the cottage, and the blackbird which sang a spring song in the blackthorn near the well, and the fox I saw basking in a corner of the field on the other side of the shallow valley . . . fooling also myself, as I walked off to see the donkeys, into pretending no winter lay ahead, no storms to prove again the omnipotence of the elements, no misadventures.

The donkeys were reliable watchmen, and their hearing was as acute as their eyesight. I have seen them many a time look up from the grass they were grazing, then stare intently into the distance with ears pricked; and in a minute or so I would find someone coming down the lane, or observe a figure moving in the moorland far away.

Penny did not, however, sound the alarm in the manner of Fred. Her voice was simply not good enough. She croaked a bray, wheezed it, producing nothing better than a strangled cry, a kind of banshee wail. Poor Penny, it was always painful to watch her frustration as she tried to compete with her son.

Fred, on the other hand, could bray so heartily that he could be heard in the next parish and beyond. Obviously this could be embarrassing when the weather was quiet, for not everyone enjoys the sound of a donkey in full cry. And so Jeannie or I would rush to him as fast as possible begging him to stop, shoving into his mouth, if we had

12

time to collect it, a large piece of bread as a gag.

At night both were usually silent. They were undisturbed by the badgers, foxes and rabbits who roamed around them on nocturnal duties. They remained sleepily serene. Yet I was sure that they would always raise the alarm if there was a stranger about, or some activity which puzzled them. I had had evidence of this a month previously.

On that occasion, a dark though clear August night, I was woken up around three in the morning by bellows from Fred. It was very still and I squirmed at the thought of the people in the neighbourhood roused by him. It was a terrible noise, and it went on and on, until I realised that something very unusual was bothering him. Then he stopped . . . and I heard voices.

On still nights we often hear the voices of the crews of passing fishing boats, sometimes the sound of voluble French from the crabbers on the way to and from Newlyn, but they soon fade away into the distance. On this night they did not fade away. And as I lay in my bed realising they had persisted for too long a time to belong to a moving boat, I knew I had to get up and investigate.

I pulled on some clothes, went outside, and shone my torch into the stable meadow below the cottage where I had left the donkeys. The light shone on Fred who was standing with his head facing towards the sea, ears upright like a V sign, displaying so intense an interest as to what was mysteriously happening that I felt like saying to him: 'Here, take the torch, go and find out what it's all about.'

Jeannie had now joined me, and we went down the path and through the white gate into Fred's field. At this moment there was a thunder of hooves behind us. The donkeys, of course, wanted to come with us, and when they found the gate shut on them Fred began trumpeting again.

'Shut up!' I said, 'shut up!' He took no notice.

At the point in the field where we were standing, we were able to look down on the sea and the shadows of the rocks below . . . and over to the left at the bottom of a castle of rocks known as Carn Barges I saw lights. I had brought my field-glasses with me, and I peered through the darkness and saw perhaps three or four moving pin-points of lights which I guessed were torches. But there were also two bright lights like those that lampers use when hunting

13

rabbits at night with their whippets. As I watched, these lights went out for a second, then on again, then out. They seemed to be signalling.

'A boat's run aground,' said Jeannie. We knew every inch of this part of the coast, and dark though it was, I could visualise in my mind the position of these lights. They came from a spur of rocks jutting out into the sea, deep water at high tide.

'It couldn't be a boat in this weather,' I said, 'there's no fog and no sea.' Then I added: 'If you stay here and calm the donkeys, I'll go ahead along the cliff path and see whether I can make contact.'

The cliff path was a rough one even in daytime. We used to keep it open for hikers by regularly walking along it with the donkeys. The donkeys loved this walk, and they would nibble the straying brambles that crossed the path, helping me therefore as I cut back brambles and gorse.

At night, however, the path was hazardous, especially if you were half running as I was doing. There were boulders on the path, and trip wires of bramble roots. Hence at one moment I missed my hold on a boulder and fell into a forest of stinging nettles, and the next I was tripped into a prickly hive of brambles and gorse. There was, too, at one point a section of low-lying elders. I hit the top of my head on one of the branches, and cut it.

By this time I was growing impatient. Who could these people be who had so aroused us! The waves, rolling on to the rocks, were surprisingly noisy; and though the torches were now several hundred yards away, I realised they might have difficulty in hearing me.

'Hello, hello,' I shouted, 'do you need help?'

There was no question of a boat being aground. The lights were on the rocks. I was quite certain of this. But I persisted with my call because I thought of no other.

'Do you need help?' I bellowed again.

No reply.

It was at this moment that I found myself in the law-abiding citizen's perennial problem. How seriously should I treat the situation? It was now half past three in the morning, and if I were to call the police or the coastguard I would have to return to the cottage, get into the car and

14

drive to a telephone box three miles away; and what would I report?

Fred's suspicions? My own doubtful ones that illegal immigrants were being landed? Or gun-runners loading a dingy? I had already scanned the sea with my field-glasses and, although seeing the lights of two vessels sailing the normal route across Mount's Bay to the Lizard, I observed no vessel close to shore. So wouldn't I be making a fool of myself if I reported curious goings on at four in the morning?

Felons galore have escaped with their sins because of doubts like mine. Once, however, when I was living in Richmond in a house facing the river just below the bridge, I acted upon my suspicions with embarrassing results.

One early morning I heard an unusual noise downstairs which seemed to come from the hall leading into the dining-room. I crept to an upstairs telephone, and informed the police that I thought the house was being burgled. Could they send a constable to investigate?

I waited for his arrival, watching for him from the bedroom window; and within ten minutes I wished I had kept my mouth shut. I suddenly realised that the house was being surrounded by a legion of dimmed torch lights. A major police attack had been mounted. And my suspicions were soon to be proved wrong.

The noise proved to be a rat gnawing a hole in the wainscoting.

The memory of this experience has always haunted me. Hence as I stood on the cliff path staring down at the strangers below me, I said to myself that I had better play safe. The men down there were probably night fishermen. It was a reasonable explanation to believe. And by believing it I would spare myself from appearing as an interfering busybody.

So I returned along the path to Jeannie and the donkeys, and to bed. Next day I learnt they were indeed fishermen . . . taking part in the Mount's Bay night fishing championship.

Fred had also given me a warning about the poacher.

One evening during the summer just before dusk, he had let out a great bellow while we were having supper. He and Penny were in the same meadow as they were now on this lovely morning; and when I had hurried down to see what was happening I found the donkeys in one meadow and a man with his back to me, shotgun raised to his shoulder, in another.

I had known the poacher had been around for some weeks because I kept finding spent cartridges at various points of the cliff. I knew, too, where he came from. He was not local though he was temporarily working in the district. And yet I had never been able to catch him in the act. Until that moment.

'May I ask,' I said gently, 'whether you have permission to shoot on this land?'

He had been about to fire, and when he swung round towards me he still kept the gun on his shoulder. He was enraged by the interruption. Indeed for a brief second I thought he was going to press the trigger. Then he turned and ran, murmuring incoherently as he did so.

On this lovely morning, however, there was no poacher. Fred's alarm note had been due to a hiker who was passing by; and by the time I arrived the hiker had unhitched his haversack and, to the donkeys' delight, was offering them buns.

'You don't mind, I hope,' he said. He was middle-aged, a round merry face, a ginger beard, and stocky. He was dressed in the manner of a hiker of all seasons. Anorak, rain-proof trousers, tough boots.

'Of course not,' I said. 'Going far?'

'Penberth, Porthgwarra, Land's End ... I may stay at Sennen Cove or go on to St Just.'

'There's a first-class hostel near St Just overlooking Cot Valley.'

'Is there? I'm a member of the Association, but if the weather isn't too bad I prefer to sleep out. I carry a tent, you see.'

'You'll find it rough going until you reach Penberth. There's no clear path yet.'

'I don't mind about that. Part of the pleasure is trying to find the way.'

Fred was wanting another bun. He was pushing his nose into the haversack, so I put out my hand and shoved him away. Then Penny tried to do the same, and I shoved her away too.

16

'Where did you start today?'

I am naturally inquisitive. I find life too short to follow the dour Englishman's policy of never asking a stranger a question. You can miss a great deal by such silence. I therefore believe the risk of a rebuff worth-while; and I was quite prepared, when I once asked a hiker a similar question, to receive the reply: 'Mind your own business.'

This time there was no hint of a rebuff.

'I got to Penzance last night, then walked through Newlyn and Mousehole and around about dusk I found myself in a kind of quarry overlooking Lamorna Cove.'

'That's the quarry which was worked at the beginning of the century and produced the stone for the Victoria Embankment in London.'

'Anyhow, it seemed isolated so I pitched my tent.'

The donkeys, aware that the haversack was out of bounds, were now a few yards off. They had found something to eat in the hedge.

'They would do well in the Pyrenees,' said the hiker, watching them, 'that's where I should be, walking along the narrow paths meeting donkeys like them. I started off from Bradford to do just that, then I got to Southampton and found myself suddenly saying I don't want to go there after all, I want to go to the far west of Cornwall where I've never been, instead.'

'Are you pleased,' I asked, 'with what you've seen so far?' I heard myself ask the question and was amused. I was putting a leading question to satisfy the ingrained wish for approval.

'Beautiful, beautiful,' he said, 'for many years I have walked all over Europe, but every year the tracks which once I knew were wild are becoming more civilised. The cult of hiking is becoming too rationalised. It has become so easy that the real pleasure of hiking is lost. You should see Austria in the summer. Tracks which I used to follow for miles on my own are now highways ... filled with perspiring holidaymakers from all over Europe. You understand, now, why I enjoyed this morning.'

'What else do you do?'

He had picked up a strand of grass and was chewing it.

'I'm a heating engineer by profession. I advise on the heating equipment for factories mostly. As you know the

17

law came in a year or two back requiring standard heat conditions for workers. That meant a lot of opportunities for someone like myself . . . and I took them up to a point.'

He paused. He was watching a French crabber with a bright green hull that had just come into view.

'But I wasn't going to let these opportunities,' he went on, 'interfere with my basic philosophy of life.'

'What is that?'

'To be free to be myself.'

I laughed.

'Those of us who feel like that are antisocial. We are told it's wrong to isolate one's personal whims from the destiny of the human race.'

'Perhaps that's today's conventional view, but it doesn't have to be the right one, and you don't have to follow it.'

'In theory you are no doubt right,' I said, 'but in practice it is hard not to be conventional if you have to earn a living.'

'Oh yes, you have to compromise.' Fred had come up to him again. He enjoyed taking part in a conversation, or rather to appear to take part. 'I compromise for that matter,' the man went on, 'though, of course, it is easier for me because I am not married and have no family responsibilities. So I stay long enough in one job to live on my savings for a year. I'm starting such a year at this moment. Thus this month I am in Cornwall, next month maybe in the Dordogne, the next in the Camargue. I'm thinking of Mexico later on. Just me and my tent, so it's cheap.' He paused for a moment, still stroking Fred's white nose. 'And what do *you* do?'

I may be adventurous myself in asking people personal questions, but I am surprised when someone asks *me* such a question. This man, however, stimulated me. He belonged to a kind of life I did not know. It is strange how often, on this wild section of the Cornish coast, I meet people who have sheered away from standard values.

'Jeannie, my wife, and I have a flower farm,' I answered, 'or perhaps I should be more accurate and say it used to be a flower farm. At one time we grew violets, wall-flowers, anemones, winter-flowering stocks, forget-me-nots and so on. Those were in our optimistic days, but one by one we had to give them up because they became too expensive to grow for the prices we received. We were quite ignorant

18

about commerical horticulture when we came here. Jeannie had been press officer of the Savoy Hotel group, and I was in MI 5, and for a long time we had to live very primitively compared to our previous kind of life. No electric light in the cottage, no running water, and the land was a wilderness, and we made many, many mistakes. At last we settled upon growing daffodils which we start picking at the end of January, and tomatoes during the summer ... those apparently empty meadows you are looking at, for instance, will be producing thousands of daffodils in February and early March.'

The BEA helicopter, bound for the Scilly Islands, came clattering along off shore a few hundred feet above the sea. It normally flew the inland route above the A.30 and Land's End. It only flew along the coast in foggy weather and so I half wondered why, on this fine day, it had come this way.

'I also write books about our life here,' I added. 'Jeannie writes too, and also draws and paints. She sells her drawings and pictures.'

'Sounds ideal.'

'Yes.'

Fred had moved away, and was staring out to sea at a passing stone boat, one of those which weekly load from the quarry at Newlyn.

'Are you apprehensive about the future?' the man asked.

'Of course. Everyone is at one time or another.'

'I didn't mean in a personal way. I meant apprehensive about the future of the environment you live in. Somewhere like Cornwall seems totally at the mercy of the advancing motorways and the millions of people who will invade you as a result.'

I did not contradict him.

'I read the other day,' the man went on, 'that seventeen million city people will be within three hours' motoring distance of Dartmoor when the scheduled motorways have been completed in a year or two. Soon after, they will be descending on Cornwall.'

'This is progress.'

'Progress to what? Nobody ever mentions that.' He paused, and then added: 'The trouble is that the population is encouraged to breed like rabbits, and the result is bound to be a plague of human beings.'

19

I smiled.

'Perhaps then,' I said, 'you will agree with the solution I have for Cornwall.'

'What's that?'

'You've heard of the lost lands of Lyonesse, the land which is supposed to have been swamped by the sea between Land's End and the Scillies many centuries ago? My idea is to have a vast sign planted in the sea with the notice WELCOME TO LYONESSE ... the drivers of the cars pouring down the motorway will see the sign, and drive on over the cliffs.'

The man laughed.

'I don't suppose the planners have ever thought what happens when the motorway reaches Land's End.'

'They haven't, nor what happens when it reaches Penzance, nor what happens to the surrounding country and coast. Cornwall is a narrow county, and there is no room for millions. But it is an age of motorway mania ...'

'And people are brainwashed into accepting it.'

'Yes,' I said.

The donkeys had returned to us. It was the haversack which appealed to them, and when the hiker picked it up and began fastening it on his back, Fred's nose once again had to be pushed away. The hiker was ready to go.

'Goodbye,' he said, and held out his hand. 'I'll think of you sometimes on my wanderings facing these problems. These problems are the same all over Europe. But you are one of the lucky ones to have privacy. Privacy is becoming the most precious commodity in the world.'

'I agree.'

'Mind you, your life wouldn't suit *me*. I wouldn't like to be anchored in one place however beautiful the surroundings.' Then he added casually, 'What do you do in the winter? Don't you find it lonely? Don't you get tired of the wind and the rain? Don't you want change?'

He was not requiring a reply. His mind was already on the next stage of his journey. He patted the donkeys, bade me goodbye, then strode away.

The haversack was irresistible. The donkeys moved away with him.

CHAPTER THREE

A girl, a secretary from Nottingham, came to the door a few days after I saw the hiker. She said she was making a sentimental journey to find Jane's cottage ... *Jane who once worked for us, then went away to live in the Scilly Isles. The girl said she admired Jane's attitude to life, the unselfconscious way she lived close to nature, her gaiety and determination. There was indeed much about Jane to admire ... only fifteen when she came to us, fair hair falling over her shoulders, a rebel against conventional schooling, wandering barefoot about her work, always sure of the standards which she wished to maintain, an elfish charm of a vagabond ... these qualities have attracted people. There had been others, before this girl, who had asked about Jane.

'She used to use those two granite steps leading to that field,' I said, pointing to a field close to the cottage, 'then over that hedge which is now covered by brambles, then across another field, over another hedge and across a further field. That way it didn't take her five minutes.'

We came that way ourselves once upon a time when there was no lane to Minack fit for a car. We turned left after

* Jane of *A Drake At The Door*.

21

passing the stone circle known as the Merry Maidens, if we had been coming from Penzance, then on past farm buildings on our left, down a narrow lane to the three cottages, all in one building, that stood high above the sea facing Boscawen Point and Logan Rock in the distance, then we drove across a grass field to our boundary hedge. We left the car there.

Jane's cottage was the middle one of the three, and she used to live with her mother, young brother, two cats, an ancient parrot, a griffin, a bull terrier, and a sheep. Once she kept a muscovy drake in her bedroom but this proved too much for her tolerant mother, and the drake was offered to Jeannie and me. I did not want it myself. I had enough responsibilities at the time without taking on any more; and so the sight of Jane arriving for work one morning with the large drake in her arms, filled me with dismay. I protested, but neither Jane nor Jeannie took any notice. They were in league together. The drake, they knew, was scheduled for the pot if it didn't find a home at Minack. So I had to be ignored; and how glad I am that they acted as they did. Boris, though only a muscovy drake, gave us much pleasure during the eight years he imposed his character upon Minack.

'It'll be easier for you to go round by the cliff,' I said to the girl, and I proceeded to explain to her the way.

The meadows she would pass, the Pentewan meadows I called them, had brought despair to us during the time we had rented them. They had been offered to us by a neighbouring farmer, and although we were occupied enough by the Minack meadows, we believed that this extra land would give us the opportunity to assure our future. Nothing of the sort. Our enterprise was to prove disastrous. We grew anemones, and the hottest late summer in years shrivelled them into dust. We grew spring onions, and twenty-four hours after the seed was in the ground a torrential downpour washed them out of the ground. We grew wallflowers, winter stocks and violets. None of them prospered; and every year, of course, we grew potatoes, potatoes which with remorseless regularity were blasted by terrible gales before harvesting time. One might have thought we would have hated these Pentewan meadows as a result, but we didn't. They provided our education in growing, made us

22

realise that the elements were always supreme however smart the human race might think itself to be, and showed us the way that if we were to be happy in this environment we had chosen, it was necessary for us to be an integral part of it. An onlooker would never belong.

The girl came back an hour or so later, and said she was surprised to find the cottages, all three of them, empty; and she wondered why they had been allowed to become so dilapidated. They did indeed look forlorn. The cottages had been built in the first part of the century for workers on the farm, but they were too remote and primitive for modern standards except for those kind of people who were refreshed by a contrast to their normal style of living; and when Jane lived there, the other two cottages were used by a schoolteacher during the holidays and a small-part actor when he was out of work. Then the Cornish farmer for whom Jane's mother worked as herds-woman sold the farm and the cottages; and the buyer was an elderly gentleman from outside the county who decided he might want the cottages for his own purposes. Hence Jane and her mother went to the Scillies, and the schoolteacher and actor found somewhere else to which they could retreat.

The cottages were, in fact, never occupied except for the rats and the mice and the occasional wanderer who sought a temporary shelter; and now a window or two were broken, and slates had been blown off the roof, and the front doors were worm-eaten and unpainted. The elderly gentleman had been forced by circumstances outside his control to change his plans; and the cottages had suffered.

There was now, however, a change to their fortunes likely to take place. The elderly gentleman had in his turn retired, and sold both the farm and the cottages. In his place there had come a modern young farmer with a keen business sense. He lived on another of his farms and needed the land, not the buildings. Thus he was prepared to sell to outsiders the farmhouse and cottages, even the old stone cowsheds as potential holiday flatlets as well. In the dreary necessity of today he had to look upon this beautiful farm as a factory, not a home.

'I met a black cat on my way,' said the girl casually, 'in fact it looked starving. It followed me to the cottages and

23

then back ... it suddenly disappeared into nowhere just by the quarry where I first saw it.'

Such information interested Jeannie and me.

'Was it fully grown?'

'Oh yes, but it was terribly skinny.'

The small quarry had been out of use for many years. Its stone once provided the base for the lanes in the area.

'It looked like Lama,' said the girl, 'except for its skinniness.'

I glanced at Lama who was lying like a miniature Trafalgar lion on a yellow cushion in the porch. A black, silky, plush figure, utterly at peace with the world she lived in. A serene example of a contented cat who was sure of the safety of each day, of a regular, well filled plate, of immediate obedience to her whims. A cat who appeared to have no reason to expect that the comfortable progress of her life would ever be rudely disturbed.

She was wild when we first knew her. She roamed the meadows around Minack one daffodil harvest time, watching us from afar, sizing us up I suppose. Ten months before, Monty, the ginger cat who came from London to Minack with us, had died; and I had then sworn, such was my sadness, that I would never have another cat. But some strange, compelling instinct forced me to hedge against this declaration, and I said to Jeannie that I would make an exception if a black cat whose home we never could trace, came crying to our door in a storm.

The cause of my unwillingness to have another cat was not, however, only due to my sadness. I had been for much of my life an anti-cat man, and although Monty was able to make me a slave my devotion was to him and not to his breed. I did not want to become involved again. I certainly did not want some kind-hearted person offering me a replacement. Monty was unique in my life, and that was that. Hence my seemingly impossible condition about a black cat coming to the door of the cottage in a storm. Hence my bewilderment when my condition was in fact fulfilled and Lama came to the door and we heard her miaow above the roar of the southerly gale and the rain.

There was, however, another condition to be fulfilled. Had she a home? Was she just a lost little black cat whose owner somewhere was grieving for her? The vet who came to see her declared she was about three months old, and at that age she could not have travelled very far. It was therefore comparatively easy to carry out our investigations, and we soon discovered that no one in the area had lost such a little black cat. Where, then, had she come from? We had our suspicions, but no reason to believe these suspicions had a base until an incident took place nearly five years later.

We had made a distant acquaintance, long before Lama appeared on the scene, with a small grey cat who wandered from time to time across Minack land. She displayed no desire to be friendly, and ran away into the undergrowth as soon as we approached her. Yet she had a strong personality, and we found ourselves taking an interest in her movements, and we would call to each other if, after an absence of a month or two, we suddenly saw her again. Jeannie gave her the name of Daisy and so, if I saw her, I would say, 'I saw Daisy this morning crossing the stable meadow.' Indeed on the morning of the day the girl called to see Jane's cottage, I had seen the compact little figure of Daisy slowly making her way up the lane. She was old now, of course, but she was still very pretty . . . and her compactness, the shape of her little head, the texture of her grey coat, all of these added up to an uncanny resemblance to Lama. Was she Lama's mother? We were sure that she was. Apart from the resemblance, there was this incident which took place nearly five years after Lama appeared in Minack meadows.

We were planting daffodil bulbs down the cliff at the time, in a meadow where we have a palm tree growing in one corner. Geoffrey was with us. Geoffrey who worked at Minack when Jane and Shelagh were here, then had to leave after a bad season when we had no money left to pay him. Then later he returned, and became a corner stone of our life; and there he was now, close to the palm tree using his shovel to plant the bulbs when he suddenly saw at the top of the meadow near the entrance of a small cave . . . a black kitten.

It was, of course, as wild as a rabbit and it darted out of sight as soon as Geoffrey approached. But we kept watch for the next few days and saw it from time to time, and we saw Daisy several times close to the cave; and there was one early morning when Jeannie crept down the cliff on her own and discovered the kitten curled asleep in the cave on a bed of dried leaves.

We had never, however, seen Lama and Daisy together. We had seen Lama *observing* Daisy on her peregrinations, but only observing. They were always at a polite distance as far as we knew ... until one evening at dusk when I had gone out to shut Boris in his house in the wood, I surprised Lama and Daisy halfway up an elm near the flower shed. They were close together, and to my astonishment there was no sign of any animosity. They seemed like two old friends having a gossip.

The following morning Jeannie asked me to fetch an onion from a string that hung in the stables, the ancient stone building in front of the cottage. I reached the doorway, the door had been left half open, and suddenly I saw on an old sack in the middle of the cobblestone floor, the little black kitten of the cliff. It was sound asleep, but such was its wild instinct that it immediately woke up to the danger of my presence and dashed to hide among a pile of old bric-à-brac at one end of the stables. There was no doubt that it was the double of Lama when she was young; and for the following ten days we had more opportunities to observe it. We used to put saucers of milk and scraps on the cobblestone floor, then watch through the window which faced the lane as the kitten cautiously emerged from its hiding place and proceeded to have its fill. The situation was certainly extraordinary ... two black kittens who had mysteriously appeared at Minack, both the same shape, both the same shape as Daisy. I think, therefore, we had good reason to believe that Daisy was Lama's mother; and that Lama had also been born down the cliff.

Then the kitten disappeared, and we never saw it again. We of course searched everywhere in the immediate area, but there was no trace of it. Nor was there any sign of Daisy, and indeed it was two months or more before we saw her pass through Minack again. We could only guess what had happened; and our guess was that Daisy had wanted to introduce her kitten into a larger world than the cliff. First, therefore, she had asked Lama in special feline fashion, if she would mind the kitten staying a while within her territory. Lama raised no objection, and indeed it had been strange to find Lama taking no interest in the stable while the kitten was there. Then, when the kitten was strong enough, Daisy decided it was time to move on. Where to?

This tantalising question remained unanswered, but it was always there at the back of our minds; and so when the girl who had gone to Jane's cottage spoke of the starving black cat she had met, we immediately wondered whether it might be the kitten grown up.

That evening Jeannie went to the quarry to investigate, and found nothing. We went together the next day, and the next, and still found nothing. I began to think the girl had imagined the incident, and decided to give up the search. Jeannie, however, remained persistent. There was a full moon the following night, and just before going to bed, while I had my bath, she announced that she was going to walk once again over to the quarry. I was lying in the bath when twenty minutes later I heard her call: 'Come here, quick!' I clambered out, wrapped myself in a towel and went into the sitting-room just in time to see Jeannie walking out of the door with a saucer in either hand. She had found the black cat, it had followed her back, and she was now about to feed it in the garden outside the porch.

I looked round for Lama and found her curled on the sofa in a tight ball. She was in a deep sleep, making a little clicking noise as she breathed, a strange little noise which was often her habit as she slept. She was therefore oblivious to what was going on outside, and I felt safe to join Jeannie in her unfaithfulness. She had already given the cat a name. Felix.

'He is starving,' she said, looking at Felix as he gulped the John Dory which had been scheduled for Lama's breakfast, 'and look at his eyes, they are glazed, he is literally dying of hunger!'

The moonlight was bright, bright enough to bathe the ancient granite rocks of the garden in an ethereal shine, though hardly enough for me to verify Jeannie's diagnosis. This was Jeannie in her exaggerating mood, I felt sure. The black cat, as far as I could see, had a long body, a bony head, a thin tail, and obviously a healthy appetite. But hardly a starving cat. If it had been it would not have jauntily followed Jeannie back from the quarry, a good ten minutes away. In any case there were plenty of rabbits for

27

it to catch on the cliffs. It was either a wild cat, or a domestic cat which had been deserted by its owner.

'Anyhow,' I said, as the cat licked the now empty plate, 'I am certain this is not a Daisy cat. It has no resemblance to her or to Lama. Far too long and leggy.'

'He is very friendly,' said Jeannie, stooping to stroke him.

There was always this fundamental difference of attitude between Jeannie and me about cats. Jeannie, from a child, had been ready to gather any cat under her protection. She represents the true cat lover, the music-hall version of the lady who will happily fill her home to overflowing with cats. I, on the other hand, was born a cat hater; and although I have now been converted by the charms of the race, I still have no wish to have more than one cat in my home. I am, in fact, still a one cat man.

I am, therefore, not a true cat lover. The true cat lover is ready to be obsequious towards any cat just in the hope of one purr in reward. The true cat lover takes no notice of those angry outbursts, those abusive remarks, that a cat makes when he is unwillingly picked up. The true cat lover queerly approaches a cat with childish cooings, and is undaunted when the cat reacts with a baleful stare. The true cat lover enjoys blissful confidence that he has a profound understanding of cats, an unfailing way with them . . . and is unabashed when a cat spits at him. The true cat lover by nature fawns upon cats.

Lama hated this cat lover's attitude. She was not influenced by flattery. If someone was mature enough to treat her as an equal, she would play fair on her part. She would respond to politeness. She would respond to admiration if conventionally conveyed. But she detested the way some cat lovers treated her as if she were an eccentric. Why do they have to gurgle like babies ? Why can't they behave with normality ? Poor fools.

'What are you going to do?' I asked Jeannie.

Felix was rubbing his bony head against her hand, and purring loudly. 'We can't have him staying around here.'

'You don't expect me to take the poor thing back to the quarry, do you?'

The poor thing was clearly enjoying himself. He was pushing his head against Jeannie's ankles, flattering her by his attention, and spurred on by his intuition that he had a cat lover on the run.

'He's not going to stay here,' I said firmly, 'we'll shut the door on him and hope he disappears by morning.'

Next morning when I awoke, I prayed that the cat had disappeared. Lama was on the bed still asleep, stretched out by my side like a black ribbon. I lay there stroking her silky back waiting for the return of Jeannie who had gone to investigate. My prayer was unanswered.

'Felix is still here,' she called from the porch, 'he's a clever cat. He made himself a nest in the shelter on an old cushion wedged between the paraffin tank and the wall.'

At this moment Lama stirred and sat up. Her day had begun. It was time for her to partake of a fish breakfast then enjoy a perambulation around the cottage. She stretched, and jumped off the bed.

'They're going to meet!' I said anxiously.

'Perhaps they'll like each other,' said Jeannie hopefully. 'Wouldn't it be fun if they did?'

'No,' I replied.

Jeannie, of course, was as anxious as I was not to upset Lama. Both of us were her slaves in a way that logical minds would disapprove of. We never went away, for instance, unless circumstances forced us to do so. The donkeys, though expecting our constant attention, had each other. Lama had Geoffrey during the day, but from five o'clock onwards was on her own. Was it our silly imagination that made us believe she might be unhappy during those long hours? And did this matter in any case? I suppose the answer lies in your valuation of trust. An animal possesses the original innocence, and is guileless in his trust. A human being, full of inhibitions, self-conscious education, and envy, is often incapable of trust; and so some pour ridicule upon those of us who love an animal. It is their loss that they do. They will never be aware of the subtle rewards we receive. The trust of an animal provides an anchor in life.

Lama had her breakfast, stretched again, then nonchalantly strolled to the porch door, wishing to be let out.

At the same moment I saw Felix at the window. His black, bony face was staring into the sitting-room.

'Heavens,' I said, 'we're in trouble.'

My voice was a moan. I sensed that if the cat was too appealing I might weaken. The pull of divided loyalties,

29

one of the most bewitching of emotions, showed signs of twisting my judgement. I had begun to feel sorry for Felix. I remained devoted to Lama. But how was I brutally to turn away a lonely creature like this cat? I longed for it to go. I needed it to go to save me embarrassment. It *had* to go if Lama's life was to be normal.

'Hop it!' I shouted to the face in the window; and it took no notice.

Such a reaction would never have come from a truly wild cat. Lama, for instance, when she was wild, never came to the window and stared into the sitting-room. This was a cat who clearly knew of the comforts a home would bring.

'If you hold Lama for five minutes,' said Jeannie, 'I'll give Felix a good feed out of sight of the cottage. That'll keep him quiet. He'll go off afterwards for a sleep.'

Lama did not want to be held for five minutes. She wanted to get out of the cottage. Quick.

'Now Lama it's for your own good . . .'

Jeannie had gone out by the back door. One, two, three minutes, and I could hold Lama back no longer. I opened the porch door and Lama stalked out, paused for a second to sniff the October air, then wandered off round the corner by the water-butt, intending no doubt to stroll slowly and peacefully down the lane to Monty's Leap where she would have a drink from the little stream which came from the wood.

Felix, however, had failed to co-operate with Jeannie. She had carried his breakfast to a spot behind the flower shed where he had eaten it, purred a little, then to show his appreciation still further he proceeded to skip his way back to the cottage. He had no wish to sleep. He wanted to rejoice at his good fortune. A home again! Someone to care for him! This was no time to waste in sleep.

And so the confrontation took place.

Plushy Lama found herself nose to nose with long-legged, skinny body, bony-faced Felix . . . and ran away in terror.

The rest of the day, it was a Sunday, was tense. Felix refused to sleep, and kept peering gleefully through the window. His charms, he seemed to think, were irresistible, and so why couldn't he be allowed inside? This was a cat of character, I regretfully realised, a cat who would be difficult to be rid of, a cat who still had confidence in the human race whatever shocks he had had in the past.

But Lama ... Lama skulked under my desk, moved to the bed in the spare room, slept fitfully, roamed the sitting-room, refused to eat, jumped on the table in the porch, stared through the glass, found Felix staring back, then uttered a frightened little cry before she jumped down and into hiding again.

By the end of the day I knew that such a situation could not be allowed to continue.

'Tomorrow morning,' I announced to Jeannie, 'the cat must go. We'll set out and find where he comes from.'

On Monday morning, therefore, we drove to our village of St Buryan and asked our friend the grocer, who had a round in the area, if he could help us. Yes, he said, he remembered a black cat at the elderly gentleman's farm which had recently been sold. The cat may have been left behind; and as the farmhouse was empty, it may have set out to find a new home. He suggested we asked the farmer who lived next door; and twenty minutes later we had the information we needed. Felix had, in fact, been left behind. The next door farmer had been feeding him, and was ready to continue to do so.

So we returned to Minack, collected Felix, put him in the car where he sat on Jeannie's lap looking alertly at the passing scene, and deposited him at his empty farmhouse, a couple of miles away as the crow flies. Then we saw the next door farmer again and he assured us that he would feed Felix every day. A kind thing to do in view of the fact he had a number of cats of his own. We were now thankful that the drama seemed to have ended, and later in the morning we went for a stroll with Lama around our meadows. She was at ease again, mistress of her own property, and the sight of her contentment gave us much pleasure.

By Tuesday midday Felix was back.

I had some trouble with the pump of our well which is some yards away from the cottage, and as I was returning after repairing it I suddenly saw Lama on the cottage roof. She was lashing her tail and looking downwards, and was plainly very angry indeed. Below her a happy Felix was waiting at the porch door.

31

'Felix,' I said coldly, 'buzz off.' And he promptly hastened towards me.

Once again we picked him up, and drove him back to the farm.

Wednesday he returned to Minack again at midday. This time Lama didn't see him; and he was away in the car while she was still sleeping on a chair in my office.

There was no sign of him on Thursday.

But on Friday morning, just as I was about to photograph some visiting friends, one of them holding Lama in her arms, another figure suddenly appeared in the view-finder.

Felix.

The maddening thing was his cocky behaviour. He was undaunted by our obvious desire to be rid of him. He felt completely at home with us. He moved around with aplomb. He was affectionate. He was certain he had a passport to stay at Minack. And so it must have been very bewildering for him why we were repeatedly picking him up, putting him in the car, and taking him back to his empty home. After all he had proved his wish to be with us. An insincere cat would not have crossed fields, and jumped over hedges, to be with us.

'Only one thing we can do,' said Jeannie, that Friday morning, 'we'll find out the telephone number of the old gentleman who had the farm, and tell him about Felix.'

The old gentleman, now retired, had moved to a house in another part of Cornwall.

'Then we can take Felix over to him.'

Once again we had Felix in the car. This time we drove to a huddle of cottages called Sparnon where there was a telephone koisk at the cross-roads. We never minded these excursions to telephone. It was a small price to pay for the pleasure of never hearing a telephone suddenly ringing in the cottage. Once upon a time each of us believed a telephone was indispensable to our lives. We now knew better. We were, for instance, now spared trivial invitations. If someone really wanted to contact us urgently they sent a telegram; and we replied by going out and ringing them up.

'You talk to him,' I said to Jeannie, when we reached Sparnon, 'you'll be more persuasive.'

One of her special charms has always been her speaking voice. It is soft and clear, and when she was at the Savoy

Danny Kaye wrote a song in praise of it, and sang it at the Palladium. I believed, therefore, that the old man would succumb to her description of Felix's plight. But she failed. I saw her in the kiosk wildly gesticulating with one hand as she talked into the receiver; and I guessed that the old man was saying that he could not have Felix with him again. His new home was no doubt too small.

'We can do what we like with him.'

She had come out of the kiosk and confirmed my guess. 'Poor Felix.'

He had been on my lap while Jeannie had been telephoning; and he had been purring away as his future had been discussed. I felt very sad for him. I felt sad for myself and for Lama. I foresaw the awful prospect of having to keep him. I could not let him be abandoned. Jeannie, I knew, would want to look after him. How on earth could I reconcile this with my loyalty to Lama?

At this precise moment a tractor and trailer came along the road we had just travelled to Sparnon; and driving the tractor was the modern young farmer who had bought

33

the old man's farm. A miraculous timing. Here was the new owner of Felix's old home appearing on the scene at the exact instant that Felix's future was being determined.

And within five minutes the future of Felix was settled. The young farmer was as co-operative as could be. He had no real cause to show any responsibility towards an abandoned cat, but he was prepared to be kind, and helpful, and anxious to solve the predicament in which we found ourselves.

'I'll take him,' he said, 'and as I bought his home I suppose I ought to look after him. We have enough cats as it is mind, but I reckon my wife will put up with another. The children will, anyhow.'

In this way the future of Felix was solved. I have never seen him again, but I gather he goes walks with the children, and on summer days he plays with them on the sands.

I wonder what would have happened to him if the girl from Nottingham had never come to Minack to find Jane's cottage.

CHAPTER FOUR

I have a dream, a muddled dream, that I live in a city again. I dream that I live in a featureless room above a car-filled street tied to a job I do not enjoy, enduring the day instead of living it. I press buttons on a cunning machine which I do not understand; and I am confused because at one moment I am obeying the orders of my company, the next of my union. Then suddenly in my dream I become affluent. I find myself imprisoned within conventional success, an important executive who is living expensively, winning applause from superiors, experiencing temporary triumphs, finding macabre fun in playing with power. A glossy, restless, hard-working, sophisticated life which provides the spur for beginners.

Then comes the end of my dream, and I am frightened.

I suddenly see myself as a disembodied person who is observing, and taking no part in the action. And I see a countryside as it was many, many years ago when it was free from man's calculated interference. There are crooked fields with the hedges still intact, and lanes sided by an

34

abundance of wild, useless beauty, lush vegetation, butter-
flies, weeds, insects, no sprays or insecticides to kill them.
Horses plough the fields, and foxes and badgers roam
wooded valleys living in earths and setts which are only
known to a local or two. New motorways do not threaten
them, nor the giant, roaring, clawing machines intent on
laying waste the land for the benefit of the factories and
beehive housing estates. The sea is clean, and rivers are
crystal clear. There is no sour sight in this romantic dream.
And yet at the end of it I am frightened.

For this paradise is beckoning me, trying to seduce me
away from my featureless room or my conventional success.
It is trying to take away from me my resolve to remain
steadfast to the present. A machine operator or a glossy
executive, I do not want to be tempted. It is necessary for
me to remain blind to any alternative way of living. I must
not allow myself to be charmed towards an existence which
is out of my reach. I must serve my sentence. I must avoid
any prospect of escape because I have insurances and mort-
gages and pension schemes, and next week I might be
promoted, and I might be able to move to a house which
will lead me upwards in the social scale. Thus I do not wish
to be distracted. I do not want to recognise the glimmer of
my inner self which yearns for truth in living. I cannot
afford to do so. And so I am frightened. My romantic dream
points to a way of life that I crave, and the chances of having
it are slipping by, and I am chained. I am conventional. I
talk myself out of taking risks. I am scared of appearing
foolish.

Then the release comes, and I wake up, and the romantic
dream is over. The great ball of the rising sun is over the
Lizard, and through the bedroom window I watch it edge
upwards inch by inch until it is out of sight, and the day
has begun. But the dream has left me with a hang-over of
disquiet. What is there for me to worry about today? Not
much. There is no great chasm for me to leap as in my
dream. I am under no pressure to hurry through the day,
no bus or train to catch, or traffic jams to infuriate me. I
have no awkward meetings to attend, and no wish to be
anywhere except in the environment of Minack. Thus the
day stretches happily before me, an ideal prospect of a day,
the perfect example of contentment that anyone seeks.

And yet there are worries to nag me. They may be trivial compared to those of other people but, because Jeannie and I live life slowly, it is remarkable how they magnify themselves into worries of irritating importance. In any case I have a temperament which is inclined to worry. I see imaginary shadows. I am unable to take happiness for granted.

There is always, for instance, the basic problem of how to earn an income from the land we have. The land is not our own. We now rent it, twenty acres all told, from an enlightened landlord who cares for the still wild stretches of the Cornish coast as much as we do; and he permits us, within reason, to be free to do what we like with the land. We have therefore been able to develop it without interference. Moreover the landlord, who comes from one of the oldest of Cornish families with large estates in various parts of the country, has thereby given us the sense of ownership without its responsibility. We never could have afforded to buy it when we first came. Indeed, like people in other spheres, we have always suffered from lack of capital; and the lack of it has been expensive.

We started out life at Minack believing that we could live on £3 a week, and expecting that stamina for hard work would alone look after our future. This naïve optimism was our salvation. Had we foreseen that our expectations were as impossible to fulfil as a cart-horse winning the Derby, we would have had second thoughts about leaving London. As it was we truly believed that we could earn enough from the land to give us a living. I do not remember what long term prospects we had in mind; for neither of us had any particular ambitions. We were not setting out to become big business flower farmers, nor had either of us any intention of writing about our experiences. We came to Minack in a mood of impractical happiness. Minack offered the roots we knew we needed, and that was enough. Minack, the most beautiful possible home we had ever found, would take care of our future. I suppose the luckiest people in the world can be the Celts who have no patience with reason.

Our beginning was also complicated by the manner with which we acquired our tenancy, for we had in fact no tenancy agreement at all. The farmer had only let us

36

occupy the cottage so as to keep out the squatters in the area; and he was not in a position to offer us a legal agreement because he was only a tenant himself. We had to wait seven years before our position was legalised; and then at last we became a direct tenant of the owner, and our security of tenure was assured. Moreover we were also allocated extra land under this agreement, cultivated land close to the cottage, and so very different from the scrub and moorland which we carved into cultivation during our first years at Minack. The land was flat, so now we also had the chance to have greenhouses.

But during the first years we had no chance of having greenhouses even had we been able to afford them. Our land was then so rough and full of boulders, and so steep, that it was impossible to find a site where the ground would be level for a greenhouse. Thus we struggled along, once we had hacked the meadows out of the under-growth, growing potatoes for May lifting; and flowers cheap to grow from seed, like wallflowers, calendulas, violets, forget-me-nots, de Caen anemones and Beauty of Nice stocks, for picking and sending to market during the winter.

These flowers, however, were not so easy to grow as one might think. Wallflowers, forget-me-nots and stocks had first to be grown in seedbeds, and then transplanted into the meadows we had prepared for them; and as the transplanting took place in mid-summer when there was frequently a period of drought, we used to find ourselves sticking the roots of the small plants in dust. Then in dismay we would watch them wilting and dying, and in panicky efforts to save them I would fill an old milk churn with water from the well up the lane (our own well water provided hardly enough for ourselves), and then proceed to dip a cup in the churn, and empty it around a plant. Of course the result was a fiasco. The dust absorbed my drop of water. The plant never had a sip.

In due course the rains came, and the surviving plants began to grow, along with the weeds. By early September the weeds were growing ferociously faster than the plants, and Jeannie and I tried hard to dispose of them in the time we could spare. At this stage of our flower farming career, however, we were often hampered by the appearance of London friends who, being on holiday themselves, thought it would be pleasant to see us again. The circumstances were now quite different. Instead of a scene in the Savoy American Bar with language like: 'What will you have?' they found us grubbing in the soil on our knees, a large basket beside each of us stuffed with weeds, in old clothes, and a desperate look on our faces which, had they correctly interpreted it, said: 'Oh, hell, the last kind of people we want to see!'

Some of these people, of course, came out of curiosity. I remember one lady whom Jeannie had always tried to avoid in London, cooing sweetly as she observed our earthy condition: 'Darlings, I'm told you're starving ... is it really worth it?' There was another occasion when an old acquaintance of mine arrived at the cottage door after bursting the exhaust pipe of his car on the way down the lane. 'Derek,' he said, admonishing me, 'you must make your entrance *civilised*.' And there was the couple, a delightful couple in the London surroundings we had known so well, who came one day and told us to wake up. We were throwing away opportunities, they said, and the man, a politician, who had been flatteringly enthusiastic over a long book I had written about the British Commonwealth, urged that I ought to stand for Parliament. Then he added, glancing at Jeannie in a flattering mood again: 'You could take Camborne in the next election ... Jeannie would win you the votes.'

Jeannie, however, was more anxious to clear the weeds and so provide the plants with the chance to produce flowers which would give us an income during the winter. But the avalanche of friends and relations continued to hinder us. Our predicament, we found, was difficult to solve. Anyone who came to see us, or wrote beforehand saying that they intended to see us, viewed themselves in isolation. Hence when they arrived to disturb us, they did not believe anyone had come before them nor did they foresee that anyone would come after them Jeannie and I proceeded to abet their self-deception by confiding in them our predicament. This, of course, was a fatal move. Our predicament, as a result, did not apply to *them*. They were the privileged few who did *not* interfere with our weeding; and so, inevitably, we were given advice. We had it often. '*Don't*,' ran this advice, 'see anyone who interferes with your work. Just tell them to *go away*.' We took this advice on one occasion, told one couple to go away along with their two noisy children; and heard echoes of our ruthlessness for a long time afterwards.

There were also those who decided to use our cottage as a base for their holiday. Our spare accommodation, of course, was very limited. Indeed it consisted at the time of a converted chicken house to which we had added a bathroom after we had sunk a well and excavated a cesspit. It stood separate from the cottage, and we used it as a depository for our clothes, as a writing and reading room (Jeannie wrote *Meet me at the Savoy* there), and as a place to bunch violets by paraffin lamp on winter evenings. Each corner of the chicken house was perched on rocks to keep it clear of the earth, and so when you moved around the room there was a hollow sound apart from the creaking floor boards. Nevertheless it offered a haven to those who wanted a contrast to their life in London; and so from time to time we would receive a pleading letter from some nerve-shattered friend who yearned for the healing qualities of the quiet Cornish cliffs.

Thereupon there was great household activity on the part of Jeannie. The weeds were left to grow except for my own lonely efforts to paw them out of the ground, while she did her best to change the chicken house into a bedroom. The red check gingham curtains were washed, the rush mats were beaten, a white cloth was placed on the trestle table to make it appear like a dressing table, and the cupboard was emptied of our clothes. If one person was coming, a narrow settee was made ready; if there were a couple, Jeannie also produced a canvas camp-bed which her father used during World War One. Then at last the tired out visitors arrived, and the cooking began.

In retrospect I marvel at our weak-mindedness. There we were struggling to survive, having to watch every shilling we spent, vividly aware that the weeds were getting the better of our plants and that the prospects of our winter income were, therefore, being remorselessly diminished ... and yet we acted as if the visitors were welcome. Good middle-class manners, I suppose. Equal good manners were displayed when we waxed over-enthusiastically about the small chicken which was contributed to the larder, or the

39

bottle which was largely consumed by the donors. Anything, for a peaceful life, it seemed. Our household bills might be quadrupled, Jeannie as unpaid maid of all work might be exhausted, my own good intentions to continue with the weeding might evaporate . . . we were prepared to make all these sacrifices in order to be bored by the brittle world we had come to Minack to forget.

'I *must* tell you about Angela. You remember how she and Robert parted . . . well, the most *fascinating* incident has brought them together again, for the moment *at least*. It seems . . .'

'George had this fabulous success at the Court, and that was that as far as Jenny was concerned. He's gone off to New York and she, poor dear, is languishing in that dreadful flat off Sloane Ave.'

'Toby was *quite sure* he was to become editor. The proprietor after all was practically having a loving affair with him. Toby was down in Sussex every week-end . . . and then of all things the *northern* editor was appointed!'

'Did you see that review of Gareth's last book in one of the Sundays? I can't remember which. It was pretty awful and Gareth was furious about it. Now he has got positive proof that Sullivan Smith who wrote it never read the book at all. He only had time for the blurb . . . and *that* came from Sullivan's girl friend who told Gareth's sister.'

'Did you hear about Caesar Downes? He stopped writing his daily column and people began to wonder whether he had been fired. But he had gone to Switzerland for one of those curious operations . . . and now he only goes out with friends of his grand-daughter!'

'We want to talk to you both seriously. Haven't you made a mistake? The Savoy are longing to have you back, Jeannie, we know that. You're a legend, people come from all over the world asking for you. Doesn't that mean something special to you? People wanting you like that!'

Certainly. She was wanted now. She had to decide how many loaves she had to bake, what there was for lunch, and how she was going to satisfy her visitors at dinner. Then there was the silver to clean, the dusting to do and because we had no electricity for a vacuum cleaner, hand brushing of the carpet. We were quite mad to put up with it.

'We've had a marvellous time. Can we come again next year?'

'NO!' I shouted in reply. I almost believed I had spoken aloud.

Good manners and truth are often enemies. One is always meeting people who boast about their frankness, and the traditional blunt Yorkshireman has established himself as a folk hero. Is he a pleasant hero? It may suit him to speak his instant thoughts without worrying about the effect they may have on the person addressed, and I even admire his moral courage, but I do not really like such bluntness. Truth, in certain circumstances, should remain hidden; and a convenient place for it to hide is behind good manners. Time is thereby gained to make more measured assessments, and these may produce more kindly results. On the other hand, as in the case of Jeannie and myself in the role of unwilling hostess and host, they confirmed the fact that we had allowed ourselves to be conned. And by midwinter we knew the price we were having to pay.

In these days various herbicides and chemical sprays keep the weeds at bay; and the saving in labour is naturally enormous. But the advantage thus gained is now often offset by overproduction, both of vegetables and flowers, and the prices obtained in the wholesale markets sometimes do not warrant the sending of the produce. This past year I have seen fields of uncut broccoli and cabbage; and acres of potatoes were only cleared because the fields were needed for another crop. The prices in the shops, meanwhile, are unaffected. The retailer has his own overheads to worry about, and he is in a position to dictate his prices. But the grower, especially the small grower, who nurtures a crop along for six months, then finds that harvest time coincides with a glut, is faced unfortunately with financial disaster. He has spent capital on producing the crop, more money on boxes or crates, and more money still on the always increasing transport costs. A retailer, or wholesaler, may have a bad week but he has the chance of recovering his losses in the following week. A grower has to wait for a year.

But when we began at Minack overproduction and consequent gluts were comparatively rare; and this particularly applied to the kind of annuals we were growing. We could rely on steady prices, high enough to cover the

41

cost of our living expenses; and there was always the chance of a bonanza if the weather up country was severe, or if there was a shortage of flowers around Mothering Sunday time. But these flowers still had to be well grown, and this was why we suffered when visitors stole our time. Plants, which for a period had been choked with weeds, could not be expected to prosper when the winds began to blow. The wallflowers were spindly, the violets small, the forget-me-nots too soft. And all because we had not had the strength of character to tell our friends to leave us alone.

We had, too, in those early days, another misfortune; and this concerned the daffodil bulbs we first bought. Clearly it was of great importance for us to stock with bulbs which would produce daffodils popular with the public. We knew nothing about the fashion in bulbs, how some varieties lose their appeal after a few years so that their blooms are practically unsaleable; and we were not aware that, as the possessors of land which had never grown bulbs before, we enjoyed a huge advantage. The land, being newly broken in, was clean of all disease; and so the chance was ours to build up a stock of bulbs which would be the envy of other growers whose land, because of years of use, had become infected with one of the bulb diseases. If, therefore, we bought clean stock of commercially popular varieties we could, even with the small amount of money we had to spare, build a foundation of bulbs which would provide us with an income for many years to come. For bulbs increase every year if they are healthy; and every so often, every two or three years is the ideal, the bulbs are dug up, sterilised, and planted again. So, like a good share, the original investment is increasing.

We asked advice from a family acquaintance who was a specialist bulb grower; and we blessed our luck that such an expert was available. It meant that we would be able to rely on him to let us have disease-free bulbs at a favoured price; and that the varieties concerned would be those most in demand in the markets. In due course the bulbs arrived. He had sent us several with charming names like Bernardino, Lucifer, Sunrise, Campanella and so on; and when they came to bloom in the spring they were as delightful as their names. Unfortunately Covent Garden did not share our pleasure. We despatched the first boxes in high

42

expectation, and indulged in the inevitable calculations as to what price they would fetch. I thought each bunch might earn us around two shillings of the old currency; and I was appalled when we received the returns and found none of the varieties had fetched more than sixpence.

We had a kindly salesman at the time called Bobby Page, who also had a club off Covent Garden which, during the war, was a home for RAF crew. These crew, when they had leave between missions, would crowd into his club, drink hard to forget, and be sure that Bobby was all the while watching over them. Bobby would find them a place to sleep, took care to see that their festivities did not stop them from returning to base, and allowed countless drinks on the slate which eventually never could be paid. Bobby was plump, and enthusiastic, and jovial, one of those who had the chance to make the lives of other people easier; and took it. But even Bobby could not be enthusiastic about the Bernardino, Lucifer, Sunrise, Campanella and so on.

'They're out of date, Derek old friend,' he wrote, 'the market long ago lost interest in them. But you can rely on me to do my best . . .'

I have a suspicion now, Bobby died some years ago, that even at sixpence of the old currency he was paying us more than the bunches were worth. He had an avuncular interest in our activities, his natural desire to help other people; and I am glad that we did not entirely let him down. Our King Alfred, the bulbs had come with the others, were superb, for instance; and we also by chance invented Cornish posies.

We began the posies because our neglected wall-flowers, anemones and forget-me-nots were not good enough to send on their own. The blooms were also scarce, and so we were at our wit's end to know what to do. One day Jeannie fashioned a dozen bunches from all the odds and ends, and sent them off in a box to Bobby, identifying them as Cornish posies. They were such a success that we were asked to send as many as possible, which was, of course, very frustrating. We just did not have the flowers to meet the demand. The following season we had more flowers available, we grew them specially with the posies in mind, and the success continued. Each posy was about the size of my fist, and Jeannie took great trouble in arranging

43

the colouring; and she used any flower that was available from November onwards. It was slow work, but the rewards were good. Then, inevitably, the posies were copied, though other growers were not the case of the competition. The florist shops were our problem. They found it cheaper to buy different flowers in the market, and then fashion their own posies. The price began to drop, and we gradually realised that the posies were taking up too much of our time and so the flower packing shed ceased to have row upon row of Cornish posies waiting to be packed. London posies had taken their place.

We were, however, left with the daffodils which nobody wanted; and this was a burden we had to carry for a long time to come. These bulbs took up space in the ground we could not spare. There was a stretch of them, for instance, down one side of the big field that ran towards the cliff; and this stretch we had created by our own hand labour from brambles and undergrowth. Hence these useless bulbs occupied favoured places; and although they were not going to earn their keep, we did not have the time to remove them. Hand digging of bulbs is a slow, lengthy business; and there always seemed something better to do than hack them out of the ground and get rid of them. So they stayed, displaying their pretty blooms each spring, bringing us financial disappointment, and so causing us much useless picking, bunching, and packing. We disposed of them in the end. My mother died, and with money she left me I financed the removal of the bulbs. They didn't go far. We scattered them all over Minack, in hedgerows and in the wood, in grassy banks close to the sea, and along the lane which leads down the hill to the cottage; and they have repaid the disappointment they caused us by the yearly, breathtaking display of their beauty; for now they are not daffodils which have to be hurried away to a distant market like Covent Garden three hundred miles away, from where they are taken to a shop, then a vase, then a dust-bin. They live out their lives now naturally, jostling side by side in unruliness; and of course my aesthetic sense is much moved.

But I cannot help wondering how much for the better our lives might have been, had we never had the need to see the sight of them. Had we been more professional, had we had capital to spare, we would not have had to rely on family acquaintances; and our virgin land would have been stocked with bulbs which could have assured us a financial future. Instead, at the very beginning of our careers as flower farmers, we moved backwards.

Did it matter? Probably not. Had we been successful at the beginning, we might have developed business ambitions. We might have become a large unit with all the worries that this entails.

As it is, if anything ever goes wrong, we will still be able to continue on our own. We hope so, at any rate.

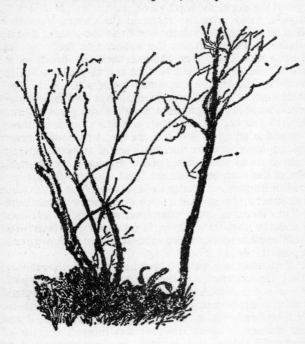

CHAPTER FIVE

We have a porch now at Minack where we sit when the cold winds blow, catching the warmth of the winter sun. It faces the small front garden and the steps that lead to the gate of the donkey field; and beyond you can see the privet hedge which hides the storage tank of the well. On the left is the door, the top half of glass, which is in fact the front door; and there are rocks in the ground outside it, making an uneven path to the corner of the cottage and the blue-painted water-butt. At this corner you look out first on to the moorland, then the sea, then the sweep of the Lizard peninsula. At night it is here that you can see the light of the Lizard lighthouse winking at you.

On the right, with its evergreen leaves and blue-mauve flowers almost pressing against the glass, is a giant veronica bush. It is too big for the small corner in which it stands, and experienced gardeners tells us that we should remove it but we leave it there for sentimental reasons. Shelagh brought it to us as a young plant, digging it up from the garden of the cottage where she lived, close to the grocer's shop in St Buryan . . . Shelagh who worked here at the same time as Jane, and who died a week after her twentieth birthday. The veronica bush therefore, reminds us of these two, and the part they played in our lives at a time when their enthusiasm was of more value than any wage we could have paid them.

Geoffrey, able as always to turn his hand to any practical job, built the foundation of the porch, first prising and inching large rocks which were in the way with the inbred skill of a Cornishman who understands stone; and his father Ken Semmens, a craftsman carpenter, designed and created the porch itself. His task was difficult because of the awkward shape, and because the framework had to be moulded securely against the old stones of the cottage around the original front door. Another carpenter had warned us, for instance, that this could not be done successfully unless the old stones were faced with a layer of cement twelve inches deep; and we both hated the sight of cement.

46

We were hoping for an old-fashioned porch which, when completed, would look as if it had been there for years. Ken Semmens created our hopes into reality, and the old stones of the cottage remained as they had always been since the cottage had been built by some crofter over five hundred years before; but Ken Semmens took his time. I was irked by his apparent lack of activity.

'How is your father getting on?' I would ask Geoffrey hopefully during the course of a day, aware that fashioning the framework would be done at home, then brought to Minack to be assembled.

'Dunno,' came the answer.

Dunno is a word that Geoffrey often uses. He delivers it in a forbidding tone on some occasions, in an impatient one on others when he considers my question a foolish one, and gently when he knows that I am seeking his help but considers, rightly, that it is not his business to become involved.

Two weeks would go by, then I would ask again.

'Any news of your father?'

I am sometimes devious in putting my questions, too devious. I desire people to catch the significance of a question without my putting it bluntly; and the result is I get no answer at all. I display the same weakness when I want some task to be performed. I am loath to give orders. I prefer to coax the person to carry out my wishes, letting his intelligence interpret my words; and so preserve a form of partnership between myself and the person concerned. Unfortunately my good intentions go astray if I make the mistake of expecting too much intelligence. I then appear to talk in riddles; and it is then that I realise that the command, 'Do this or do that', can provide a relationship sounder than that of partnership.

Another week or two.

'I expect we'll be seeing your father soon?'

Afterwards, when the porch had been completed, I was ashamed of my impatience. I had succumbed to the contemporary mood of expecting instant results. I was chivvying a craftsman, a Cornish craftsman at that, to hurry his work. I was behaving like a brash city newcomer with no experience of country life; and I was startled that an attitude which I thought I had long buried, had popped up again.

47

'I was thinking,' I persisted, 'that the porch might be ready by Christmas.'

Geoffrey was having his croust, the Cornish equivalent of a tea break, in the shed which we once used for bunching and packing daffodils. He was sitting in a canvas chair with a chaffinch at his feet, a tom tit, and a couple of blue tits. These birds and others waited impatiently for his croust breaks, and at week-ends when he was at home, they fluttered in annoyance beside the closed door.

'Is there any chance?' I added.

He looked at me as if I were a spoilt child, took a bite at the cake he was holding in his hand, and replied, mouth full:

'None at all.'

Unlike myself, Geoffrey was usually direct in his speech. I might disagree with him but I always knew that he was speaking the truth as he viewed it. I therefore could not feel offended when he was blunt. He saw no purpose in wasting time in *finesse*. He saw a problem in black or white, a solution in the same colour. He did not allow his judgement to be cluttered by a permutation of pros and cons. And I envied him this quality.

'Oh,' I said doubtfully, 'I'm sorry about that.'

I was naturally curious to find out why, but there again my timidity got the better of me. I did not dare intrude into the world of Geoffrey and his father. I was prepared to prod but was too apprehensive to do more; but to my surprise, Geoffrey on this occasion showed none of the reticence I expected of him; and without requiring any urging from me proceeded to explain the reason for the delay. The explanation was so simple that I marvelled at my stupidity for not extracting it before.

Condition of the timber was the reason. I had imagined that the necessary timber had only to be bought at the timber yard for the carpentry to begin; and this is the case in many sections of the carpentry trade. But Geoffrey's father had different ideas. He was suspicious of all timber for sale, and when he went to the yard he would poke around for hours, looking at this piece of wood and that, feeling it, dismissing it, taking as much care before making his choice as a jeweller sorting out gems.

Nor was he content with his choice once it was made;

and hence the delay to our porch. He sought perfection, and although the timber he had chosen was in his opinion the best available, it still had to be *dried*. Present day timber is in so much demand that it is scarcely out of the forest before it is in the workshop. And so it is immature, green and sappy, and no good for a master craftsman.

Thus I learnt that the timber Ken Semmens had chosen for our porch was in a workshop where a paraffin heater was burning day and night, a slow method of drying I would have thought, but the only method which was possible; and the timber was shifted this way and that, so all parts of it had the benefit of being close to the heater at one time or another. Such dedication to perfection is the route to a masterpiece; and though a humble porch could never enter the rating of masterpieces, Ken Semmens's porch certainly has one claim to fame. No part of it has ever leaked despite the battering it has had from the rain and the gales. The wood had been dried. The joints, as a result, have never shrunk. The craftsmanship had been perfect.

So although we had hoped for the porch by Christmas, it was worth waiting . . . till after Easter.

We sit often in the porch in daytime during the winter. A banquette runs the length of the little garden side. Opposite, between the door into the sitting-room and the end where the veronica bush presses against the glass, there is a small settee made of bamboo and cane. It is placed alongside a small natural wood table, the shape of a miniature refectory table though large enough to seat five; two on the settee, two on the banquette, one on a bamboo chair facing the veronica bush. Jeannie, when we are alone, generally sits on the banquette, and up above her through the glass roof, she can see Philip the gull passing time on the chimney. Or he will flap his wings and stare imperiously at her so that she is impelled to fetch a piece of bread and throw it up to him. I, on the settee, meanwhile am forced into awareness that the donkeys are demanding my attention. There they will be in the corner of their field just above the little garden, head beside head, white nose beside white nose, two pairs of solemn eyes watching my every move, driving me in the end to exclaim: 'For goodness sake, donkeys, do look at something else!' It is at

49

such a moment that they know they have won. Penny will nudge Fred, and Fred will paw the ground. They know that it will be only a matter of minutes before I will leave the porch and attend to their wants. Move to another field? No. Chocolate biscuits? Yes. Well here you are. Anything for quiet.

We were to have another creature that winter, staring at us through the glass. A racing pigeon who had tired of racing. At first we took little notice of it as it hung around the neighbourhood of the cottage, sometimes huddled on the roof, sometimes perched on a jutting stone in the building we call a garage, sometimes squatting on the grey chippings while Lama watched it from a distance. For the temporary presence of a racing pigeon was not unusual. Racing pigeons, wayward racing pigeons, like to pause at comfortable homesteads if they find themselves in the mood. Maybe a young bird has lost its way, and needs a rest to regain its nerve; or perhaps it is an old bird, now cynical about the purpose of racing and expending so much effort. In either case they do not normally stay long, a week or two at the most. Then off, refreshed, flies the young bird to search for his distant loft; and the old bird, resignedly, sets off for his.

Neither, alas, are likely to be welcomed on their return. Pigeon fanciers require sensible, obedient birds, conventional birds, who will hurry back to their timing clocks without taking a holiday on the way. Pigeons, therefore, who pause at Minack are asking for disgrace; and, indeed, on two occasions when we traced the owners of errant pigeons by the identification ring a pigeon carries on its leg, we were told we could keep them. On a third occasion we traced the owner to Dublin; and were informed that although it is in order for a pigeon to fly direct to Ireland from the despatch point, it cannot be imported in a normal manner for fear of it carrying the germs of foot and mouth disease. Hence our offer to return the bird by rail and boat was misguided. The owner would have to bear the expense of quarantine, and he had no intention of doing so. He told us to kill the bird. We didn't of course, and one day, a week or two after we had received the letter, it flew away. Back to Dublin? I hope not.

We had learnt, therefore, to keep secret the presence of a

racing pigeon at Minack. Not that it was ever easy to discover its identity, because a pigeon is so elusive, as elusive as any bird, if there is no loft. Indeed when we decided that we would never again try to trace the owner we were relieved our chasing days were over. Our contribution to a pigeon's welfare was now limited to scattering grain periodically on the ground and making sure it had water available. Thus is could rest with us, feed, and fly away when it felt inclined.

Lama, meanwhile, viewed each visitor with interest; and although the phrase 'cat among the pigeons' has a fearsome ring about it, Lama's interest was not fearsome. She would settle a few yards from a visitor, crouching on the ground and staring, while the visitor unconcernedly pecked for the grain. The visitor was never in any danger of attack. Lama, except once when she swiped with her paw at a chaffinch which was annoying her with its monotonous call a foot away from where she was trying to sleep, has never attacked any bird. It is one of her charms that she has no inclination to do so. One of the charms, too, of Monty who was her predecessor. Neither wished to kill birds. I am sure I would have had a different attitude to both of them if they had.

Sometimes one of the visitors would be fascinated by Lama instead of Lama being fascinated by the visitor. There was one heavily-built racing pigeon with the colouring of a wood-pigeon who was so intrigued by Lama that he would keep following her about as if she was a guide in the strange place in which he found himself. Lama would set off on a philosophical stroll down the lane towards Monty's Leap, and this heavyweight pigeon would promptly swoop off the cottage roof where he had been perched, fly imperiously for a moment or two overhead, then land a few feet in front of a startled Lama who, until that instant, was only intrigued by rustling noises suggesting possible mice in the grass on either side of the lane. This pigeon would then strut self-importantly in front of her, cooing; and when Lama failed to do whatever it was he expected her to do, he took to the air again but with such a noise that his wings sounded like castanets in the sky. Lama continued her stroll unperturbed.

Once I found a racing pigeon lying near Monty's Leap

in the lane, and at first I thought it had broken its leg. I picked it up and carried it to the coop we had for injured birds and which we kept in the small greenhouse. We soon realised that its legs were uninjured, and that instead it was suffering from concussion. It had been a foggy morning and so, I presume, its in-built radar system must have gone astray and it had crashed into a tree when it believed it was flying in the open sky. I was told later that this was not unusual; and that if, in a cross Channel race, the leader of a group of racing pigeons lost its sense of direction in a fog and flew into the sea, all the other pigeons would follow.

Anyhow our concussed pigeon slowly recovered its balance, staying for over three weeks in the coop before we considered it was well enough to be let out; and even then we still kept it within the confines of the greenhouse for another week or so. It was now, of course, very tame, and we naturally became fond of it, so by that time we had given it a name and, guessing it was a male, we called him Percy.

Percy, in pigeon fancier's parlance, was a blue chequer which is very similar to a rock-dove, ancestor of the racing pigeon. We have rock-doves in our neighbourhood, and a pair has from time to time nested insecurely on a ledge in a cave which leads from the pool where we swim in summer time. I say insecurely because the ledge is safe when the weather is normal and the sea below is quiet ... but if a gale blows up the cave becomes a cauldron of huge waves and spray. Moreover this pair of rock-doves had the habit of nesting late, and I used to see young in the nest as late as October when the great gales of the autumn were due. Poor foolish rock-doves. The young never survived those gales.

Nor, I am afraid, did Percy survive his stay at Minack. When we let him out of the greenhouse, let him be free, he had completely recovered and the opportunity was his to fly away to any destination he wished. Instead he decided to stay in the neighbourhood, and though occasionally during the day he would fly off on a voyage of investigation, he spent most of his time close to the cottage; and at night, the door of the greenhouse left open for him, he would go inside to roost. After a few weeks we were so accustomed to his presence, so accustomed to the complete trust he seemed to have in us, in Geoffrey, in Lama, and even in the strangers

52

who called that we began to take it for granted that he would be staying with us forever. Then one day there was no sign of him, nor the next day nor the next.

A week later I was in one of our meadows overlooking the sea. It was a pleasant morning, hazy, and the *Scillonian* which was passing on the way to the islands, crowded with holidaymakers, hummed through the quiet water like an elegant yacht. This was a trip I thought, that the holiday-makers would enjoy. No seasickness today. A voyage so unlike those turbulent voyages of winter, a southerly gale sweeping across Mount's Bay, bigger vessels than the *Scillonian* hurrying for shelter, yet the *Scillonian* herself always keeping to schedule, lurching and plunging, making me thankful to be on land as I watch her pass.

I was in this meadow, wondering what we could grow in it. The meadow had always been unsatisfactory. Over the years we had tried potatoes, anemones, stocks, wall-flowers, lettuce, and more recently daffodils; and none of them had produced crops which were worth the work involved. I had had the soil analysed, and there had been no sickly revelations. Pundits had suggested this and that to no avail, and I had reluctantly come to the conclusion that the only course I could take was to leave it fallow. It was a pity because it was a pleasant meadow facing south, and large by our standards; and I felt frustrated by my conclusion. Hence I would wander off to the meadow from time to time to stand and wonder, an idle, fruitless game of imagining lush crops which might bring in the cash.

As I stood there I suddenly saw a scattering of feathers beside a rock in the corner of the meadow. It was not unusual, however, to see such feathers. A hawk may have pounced on a blackbird or a thrush, or it may have been the peregrine falcon which haunts this coast which had made the attack, or was it a fox who had had a meal? I looked at the feathers from a distance, sadly but without involvement, when some instinct urged me to go closer. I reached the rock, knelt down and picked up a feather, holding it for a moment in my fingers. I will never know the truth of what had happened. That is the trouble when one lives close to nature. There are always so many unanswered question marks. It is impossible, as in urban societies to pretend to be knowing.

All I can say is that the scattered feathers were blue and white; and we never saw Percy again.

The new pigeon had arrived at Minack later than usual, in the middle of October, long after the racing pigeon season had ended. There was the customary identification ring on one leg, and a second ring, denoting that at some time in the previous weeks it had been taking part in a race. It was a very pretty pigeon, more delicately built than the previous ones we had known. Officially it would have been called a red pied pigeon; and a red pied pigeon is one whose colouring is partly brick-red, partly white. Of course there are many variations, and I have since seen a red pied which was more white than red, and another which would have been all red except for a streak or two of white. But the colours of our new pigeon were nicely balanced, and its general appearance was admirable. Its only fault, if this was a fault, was a patch of white on its head which made it look comic. So comic, in fact, that Jeannie was reminded of the old-time music-hall performer called Nellie Wallace. Nellie Wallace had a bird-like face and made a habit of wearing funny small hats; and this patch of white on the pigeon's head looked, to Jeannie, like one of those hats. Our new pigeon now had a name. Nellie.

Nellie, at first, was just another pigeon who would soon be off and away, and we paid no more attention to her than was our habit towards intinerant pigeons. We gave her grain and water, made some remark when we passed her, and waited for the day when she would no longer be with us. Gradually, however, as the weeks went by she began to impose her personality upon us, and impose it on others as well . . . Lama, the gulls on the roof, our local chaffinch, robin, blue tits, and the dim little dunnocks. All of us became aware that we were in the company of a Presence. I began to find myself, for instance, stopping to talk to her, instead of passing her by with a casual remark. I felt she expected me to do so, and I did not want her disapproval. Her attitude towards Lama was equally compelling. Lama, who at first treated her with polite curiosity, was startled to find Nellie behaving in a bold, challenging fashion towards her. Lama, curled in a niche of rock sheltered from the wind by the porch, dozing, would suddenly wake up to find Nellie advancing towards her ejaculating: 'Coo,

54

coo, coo!' . . . as if she was meaning: 'Boo, boo, boo!' The small birds received similar provocative attention, and they soon found it unwise to attempt to snatch a grain or two from the handful we had scattered on the ground for Nellie; for she would dart at them in greedy fury. As for the gulls on the roof, their lazy dignity was made to look foolish when Nellie, in a dashing sweep from the sky, decided to join them. For no valid reason she would jostle them away from the spot they had chosen to survey the scene below them; and, except for Philip, they would surrender their positions without argument. Philip, our oldest gull on the roof, would never budge. He would stare at Nellie, then open his wide beak. Nellie never made the mistake of testing his intentions.

Her favourite place, we soon learnt, was the glass roof of the porch. Why it should have been so appealing to her I do not know but whenever it was fine there she would be, sitting on the glass directly over our heads. Presumably she wanted companionship. Or perhaps it amused her to keep an inquisitive eye upon us. In any case while I, from my seat, would look up and see her squashed, feathery underparts, Jeannie on the other side of the table faced the funny, Nellie Wallace head ... and a beady eye. She was often to watch us from this vantage point during the winter months.

CHAPTER SIX

The rains came in November. They came roaring in from the south, grey skies, grey seas, water-butt overflowing flushing a channel in the grey chippings, pools on the stone path outside the door, donkeys with heads down and backs to the weather when they could be dry in the stable, land soggy, noisy restless trees, birds sheltering in the escallonia by the terrace we call the bridge, a gull clinging in the wind to the roof, all nature accepting the first punishment of winter.

Then suddenly a day, and the sky is blue brushed by fluffy white clouds, and it is unexpectedly warm, and I forget. Momentarily yesterday's storm is only in the imagination. We have a day lent. The Indian summer continues.

On such a day I began the annual inquest into our efforts. I was sitting at the table in the porch, Nellie on the glass above, invoices and price returns around me, in a serious mood, prepared to study details which my lazy nature would have preferred to avoid, expecting Jeannie to join me; and there was no sign of her.

'Jeannie!'

No reply.

I become mildly irritable when, after deciding to perform some task which I do not wish to perform, some factor hinders me from immediately starting it. I may have decided, for instance, to pay bills and I am ready to carry out the unpleasant task, my cheque book at hand, the bills staring at me; and then I discover I have run out of envelopes. Or

I may have decided to spend the morning writing, locked in the old stable which is my office, quite undisturbed, determined to concentrate on my work instead of letting my mind wander; and an overnight telegram is delivered with the post . . . will I ring so-and-so by midday?

'Jeannie!' I called again. 'What are you doing? I've got everything ready.'

My voice, from the porch, carries easily through the cottage. There is only the sitting-room, the kitchen, our tiny bedroom with its windows facing Mount's Bay, the spare-room which we bought as a chicken house, and the bathroom. All on the ground floor.

The sitting-room is thirty-five feet long. On the left, as you look into it from the porch, is the end wall on which hangs a wistful portrait of Jeannie by the Polish artist Kanelba. Below, to the left, is the gap prised out of the three-foot-thick stone wall which leads to the converted chicken house. Here at this end is the widest part of the sitting-room, fifteen feet wide. It is here that I have my veneered walnut kidney-shaped Regency desk which was given to me by my father and mother as a wedding present; and here, too, is the small, oak gate-legged table where we eat when it is too cold to be out in the porch, sitting on Windsor chairs which we brought with us from London. Beside my desk beneath the window is a storage heater which has solved the damp problem from which old Cornish cottages suffer; and then comes the hi-fi radio and record player, and next to it is an eight-drawer mahogany tallboy which had been for many years in Jeannie's family, then bookshelves. There are other bookshelves beneath Jeannie's portrait behind me to my right as I sit at my desk: and directly behind me is a corner oak cupboard, top half with three shelves and a glass door, which came from my old family home of Glendorgal near Newquay on the other side of Cornwall. I remember this cupboard as a little boy. It is of Dutch origin, and there used to be kept in the top half a weird collection of Indian doll-like figures which my father had brought back with him after touring the world as a young man . . . a sepoy in Indian Mutiny uniform, a turbaned Sikh, a Pathan with a magnificent flowing black moustache, a Ghandi-like figure naked except for a loin cloth, an extravagantly dressed figure which

57

I believed to be a Maharajah. They were all gaily coloured, very small and beautifully made, and yet they seemed to me to be slightly menacing. I can only guess why I felt like this; I suppose it was a childish fear of the unknown. But the cupboard, in contrast, gave me a sense of security. It was a simple design without frills, and it caught my imagination, and this is the reason why it is at Minack today. Known as Derek's cupboard, it came inevitably into my possession after my parents died.

At the other end of the sitting-room there is a black enamel stove, to the right of an old oak dresser, which provides an open fire if you pull up the mica-covered front; and it is set in an alcove. A black enamel pipe climbs from the stove up the back of the alcove and disappears into the ancient chimney, and it looks unusual. So unusual that I explain to those who remark upon it that the stove is Swedish ... and immediately there are knowing murmurs of appreciation. It does, in fact, look as if it might be Scandinavian, one of those sturdy, practical stoves which conjure up a picture of cosiness on snow-filled winter nights ... but it is an ordinary British stove. Nothing, except for the pipe, unusual about it at all.

The alcove is our own creation, or rather we have re-created it because there is no doubt it existed there before. In those days the alcove would have served as an open fireplace, and the crofter who lived in the cottage would have kept the fire burning with furze from the surrounding moorland, and quantities of bog turf. Here then was his hearth, and where his family cooked with the aid of those strange utensils like the Cornish kettle, not the customary kettle but an iron bowl with three legs in which stews and vegetables were cooked by the heat of the furze flames. I found such an iron bowl not long ago half-buried in a hedge nearby.

But when we first came to the cottage the hearth had been filled in and faced with plaster; and a battered, rusty Cornish range showed that the old-time method of cooking had been given up years ago. The Cornish range was far too decrepit to use, and we took it out and substituted an inexpensive cooking stove we bought in Penzance. Then later we took that out, too, and had an Esse instead; and it was when we were installing this Esse that we discovered the 'cloam' oven.

This oven was, of course, as old as the crofter's hearth and it would have been in use since the days the cottage was built. It was shoulder-high on the right of the hearth, and had a slab of granite as its floor, then a dome made up of small stones ... thus making a circular space like the inside of an upturned cup. The entrance, on the hearth side, was less than two-foot square, and when the oven was in use this was blocked by large stones kept handy on a ledge. First, however, the oven was stuffed with furze and wood and set ablaze; then when it was judged to be hot enough, the embers were swept out into the hearth, the food placed inside, and the entrance tightly fitted with the large stones. In this way centuries of baking took place in this oven.

News of the discovery of this Minack antiquity quickly circulated. The mason who made the find came from Mouse-hole, and from Mousehole the news was carried to Newlyn, and within a few days I was having a haircut in Penzance when I was startled to hear the barber remark: 'Congratu-lations ... I understand you have found a cloam oven at your place.' Such is the interest of the Cornish in things ancient.

Then one day we saw the vicar coming up from Monty's Leap towards the cottage. He was an old man, much res-pected in the district, and known in a wider sphere as an authority on West Cornwall ancient monuments. We ourselves, when we saw him through the window, believed he was making an evangelical call upon us; and there was a flurry of picking up magazines and newspapers, shaking of cushions, and other activities that take place when an unexpected visitor suddenly descends upon one. He arrived panting at the door, he had had a long walk, and I greeted him warmly.

'How nice to see you, Vicar,' I said, still blind to the reason for his visit, 'do come in. We were just making ready a cup of tea.' My mind, meanwhile, was wondering how to explain to him that solitude in a meadow overlooking an ungovernable sea was more spiritually uplifting to me than a disciplined service shared by a duty-bound congregation.

I had no reason to concern myself.

'I have come,' said the vicar gasping, 'to see your oven.'

In due course electricity was brought to the cottage; and it was then that Jeannie decided she no longer wanted a fuel stove to cook by; and so the Esse was removed and the new stove, the Scandinavian pretending stove, was substituted. Meanwhile she had designed, after much research into the kind of kitchen she was looking for, a kitchen which was like the galley of a yacht. It had to be like a galley, because there was no room for anything else.

It faces the sitting-room door into the porch, an oak chest on one side of the door, a large settee with its far end close to the alcove on the other. It is seven foot long, and there is only a two-foot space between the cooker, sink and refrigerator, all set against the wall . . . and the table-high top of a cupboard where Jeannie prepares her dishes. Cupboards are a remarkable feature of the kitchen. There are, indeed, thirty-six cupboard doors, and the carpenter who made them, a boatbuilder from Newlyn, jokingly said afterwards that he would never forget the experience. They are in natural wood with black hinges, and they range in size from a comparatively large one which holds such things as a mop and a long-handled duster, to the small ones which climb up the ceiling in which china, glass and stores are kept. Every inch, therefore, of the kitchen is made use of, yet crowded though it may sound, there is an attractive airiness about it. One end is open to the sitting-room, except for a waist-high door like the bottom half of a stable-door; and then there is a special feature, a large window-like frame without glass, which was Jeannie's brightest idea. This window is set in the centre of the kitchen, facing the porch. So if you are standing in the porch, or in that part of the sitting-room, you can see into the kitchen; but you will do so through the contents of a bowl of flowers. For it was part of Jeannie's idea that a window frame containing a bowl of flowers would help to make the kitchen a part of the sitting-room without it having the severity of an open-plan kitchen; and the idea has been much admired. Thus there is the kitchen and its cupboards and its equipment on one side of the window, while on the other there are pictures hanging on the wall and two rows of bookshelves below them.

Our bedroom, our box-like bedroom, is only a yard from the kitchen. It is so small that the one who lies on the far side of the bed has difficulty in getting there, and usually climbs over the other to do so. But tiny though the bedroom is, it is a very beautiful one. The walls are of the original rough stone painted white and the ceiling is papered with a Werner Graaf design of pink dianthus and lime-green leaves. There is just enough space for a William-and-Mary chest of drawers, and a little walnut desk, like a school desk, where Jeannie keeps her papers. The two windows are curtained with material of the same pattern as the wallpaper. One window looks down the lane towards Monty's Leap, and in winter when the elms are bare of leaves I look out on the fields on the other side of the shallow valley; and as I lie there, head on pillow, I sometimes watch a fox at first light trudging back to his earth on the cliff after a night's hunting. The other window faces east to the Lizard, and when the visibility is right a flick of light every few seconds comes blinking across the thirty miles of Mount's Bay. I count these flicks, if I am trying to sleep, as other people count sheep.

The spare-room, the converted chicken house, is also papered with a Werner Graaf design, both ceilings and walls; and so, too, is the bathroom, with all the windows curtained to match. There are table-high fitted cupboards along one side of the spare-room; and on the other side, the three windows, through which the chickens were expected to look out, are still there, though the frames themselves are, of course, different. A tall, old-fashioned wardrobe is also still there, one which we managed to squeeze through the door of the chicken house when we first erected it ... but, because of the transformation, it is now impossible to move out. You would not now think it had ever been a chicken house; and the outside is disguised by the cedarwood tiles which cover the roof and the walls.

The cottage, therefore, is small enough for a shout easily to be heard. And yet Jeannie didn't reply.

'Jeannie!' I called once again, then began impatiently to gather up my papers, the invoices and the price returns. If *she* wasn't interested, I wasn't either. This unreasonable action on my part was accompanied by a coo above my head. Nellie, still squatting on the glass roof, was perkily

61

looking about her. I scarcely took notice of her. Let her coo. I was too concerned with the destruction of my good intentions.

Then suddenly Jeannie appeared. From *outside* the cottage, not inside. And Nellie stopped her cooing.

'Where on earth have you been?' I said crossly. 'I have been waiting for you all this time . . .'

My harshness was misplaced. I was making a fool of myself. I could see it in the way she looked at me.

'The water has gone again!'

This was something more vexing than wrecked good intentions.

'Oh hell,' I said.

'There's nothing coming into the washing-machine.'

She had slipped out of the back-door, while I had been waiting for her, with a bundle of washing, taken it down to the hut where we keep the machine, then waited for the tub to fill. It hadn't.

We are not on the mains. The mains were brought a few years ago to the farm buildings a quarter of a mile away up the hill; and we had the chance of having it brought down to Minack. We did not take it because, apart from the expense involved, we preferred the flavour of our own well water. The well, thirty feet deep and sunk on our behalf by two miners from St Just, provided water which had the freshness of a mountain stream.

Unfortunately the well was not deep enough. The dowser prophesied we would have plenty of water at fifteen feet. It wasn't there. Nor at twenty, nor at twenty-five; but at thirty a great shout went up from all concerned when water began gushing into the splendid base of the hole which had taken so much of our money to reach. So much money, in fact, that there wasn't any left that year to pay for a pump to pump it up.

In retrospect, I realise, I should have asked the miners to go still deeper, or alternatively to widen the base so that it became a small reservoir catching the seeping veins of water around it. Hindsight, however, can be deceptive. Hindsight is inclined to ignore the mood and circumstances of the time concerned, dwelling instead on the logical steps one might have taken. Hindsight relies on the evidence of memory, and memory often forgets the influence of emotion.

Thus, when the miners struck water, we had become so emotionally exhausted by the weeks of waiting, of collecting and returning them to and from St Just, of the periodic explosions as they blasted the rock, of the laborious hand drilling, of the slow clearance of the debris, and our anxious efforts to find the money to pay them, that we were only too thankful to say goodbye to them, kind and enthusiastic though they had been. Water had been found ... so next year, we hoped, we would have the money to pump it into the cottage.

And we did. The following year the water came flowing into the cottage, and we had the same pleasure of turning on a tap as some primitive couple who had never seen one before. Washing up became conventional. Hot water, heated by calor gas gave us the experience of baths again and we wallowed in them instead of washing in sea water among our rocks, or trying to manage in an old-fashioned hip-bath helped by a couple of kettles warmed on the stove. We were now as comfortable as if we were in one of those Savoy suites we knew, glorious deep baths after full days, and made the more pleasurable after the Spartan past. Unfortunately at the beginning of October the water in the well began to disappear. Gasping, air-locked pipes took the place of rushing water. The storage tank was empty. The pump which filled it had nothing to offer.

The situation is repeated annually. Wet or dry summers make no difference. Wells, it seems, are compelled at that time of year to take a holiday; and as they show the signs of becoming lower and lower, well-owners share a comradeship with each other like old soldiers.

'How's your well?' I will ask another well-owner; and immediately feel comforted when he confides that he is greatly concerned.

Or I would put a feeler in a more devious way.

'My well is doing very nicely this year. Hardly any trouble as yet.'

'You're damned lucky,' I would gleefully hear in reply, 'mine has never been lower.'

I have mitigated some of the inconvenience by making use of another well several hundred yards away up the lane, a well from which previous inhabitants of the cottage used to fetch their water in pails, and lead their cattle to drink in a neighbouring trough. It is a surface well, about three foot deep, and it was shared by us for some years with our friend Bill who keeps one of the farms at the top of the lane. He needed it both for his cattle and domestic purposes while I, in the summer, used it to water the tomato plants. It was not, however, a vigorous well. It never went dry but it was very slow to fill; and so if I used too much for the tomato plants, Bill was put to considerable inconvenience; or, alternatively, if he obtained the water his house and cattle required, the tomato plants went thirsty.

Bill is now on the mains, which means we have full use of the well; and we do so in two ways. The overflow, for instance, takes a winding route in a ditch, underneath the lane in a pipe, through a copse and along the top of the greenhouse field and down the side bordering the wood, then through a gap close by the small orchard and continuing secretly some yards among boulders until it enters the lane at the spot known as Monty's Leap. Then it crosses into a patch of ground which we are always intending to make into a water garden, though a hole in the hedge until it finally reaches the reservoir . . . a small reservoir which we dug out with shovels so as to provide a plentiful supply of water for the tomatoes.

Now this may appear to be an ideal arrangement; and so it would be, both for the tomatoes and as a reserve supply for ourselves, were it not for the fact that this lane well can also become so weak that only a trickle overflows, only a trickle runs along the ditch and into the reservoir which, in a rainless period, is barely covered by more than a foot or so of water. Nor is the water as clear as it might be; and it is certainly not suitable for a washing-machine.

Hence we have another method of tapping the well. We syphon it. You can do this if the well is higher than where you want the water delivered; and so we have an alkathene pipe with an end stuck in the well, carrying the water down hill to the tap at the other end. Thus the overflow water moves day and night into the reservoir, while the piped water is used on special occasions.

One special occasion is when the cottage well begins to fail, and is only able to pump thirty or forty gallons a day. There upon we move a hundred gallon tank alongside the reservoir, fill it with clean water through the alkathene pipe, then use the reservoir pump to pump it up the hill to the fixed tank adjoining the cottage well. This sounds complicated, and it is. I have to keep a cool head.

We still use, for instance, the cottage well for drinking water, switching the electric pump on and filling a couple of large jugs direct from the pipe that rises from the bottom of the thirty foot hole . . . but we used the fixed tank for the supply of all household needs, including the washing-machine. It is therefore my duty to see we have drinking water from one source, and that one tank fills the other for our household needs. But how do I remember to do this?

I don't. I may remember in the morning to fill the first tank, the tank by the reservoir, then see that the contents are pumped into the second tank, the tank by the cottage well . . . but I don't remember to keep a check on the situation during the day. Suddenly, therefore, I hear a cry from Jeannie, a cry like the one I heard as I was mooding over the invoices and price returns.

'The water has gone again!'

In civilised places one becomes so soothed by the availability of necessary services that one takes them for granted, like wearing trousers or a skirt. And when there is a breakdown in the conventional routine, the failure of a loaf to be delivered or the morning newspaper, or the daily bottle of milk, there is such astonishment that the mishap is certain to attract the attention of newspapers and radio. Highly paid ladies and gentlemen will interview housewives whose world has been turned upside down by the striking breadmakers or milkmen or delivery vans; and millions of people, either seeing the news or reading it, will devote their minds for a minute or two to the disaster which has befallen this section of the supermarket civilisation.

'The water has gone!' said Jeannie again.

'I heard . . .'

It was maddening that in November, after such a deluge of the last few days, we should be thirsty for water. Water was everywhere, and mud . . .

It was strange, too, that Jeannie, who has such intelligence, who held the top girl job of her time in London, who has written two books including *Hotel Regina* which a critic described as better than Vicki Baum's *Grand Hotel* . . . was mentally incapable of understanding the

65

sequence of actions which filled first the reservoir tank then the cottage tank, then the washing-machine or anything else. For years I had tried to explain the position ... then long ago I gave up. I always did the job myself.

'All right, darling,' I said on this occasion, meekly, 'I'll see what I can do'

I walked down to the tank by the reservoir and turned on the tap of the alkathene pipe, then I came back to the cottage waiting for it to fill Syphoning was not a quick job. The water flowed at the rate of seventy gallons an hour.

'Remind me,' I said to Jeannie, 'that I've turned it on.'

'I'll get the buzzer.'

The time buzzer, the lifebelt of forgetful people.

'How long?' she asked.

'An hour.'

Inconveniences, however, can enhance the pleasure of living. We have never bemoaned our isolation because we are cut off from much of the floss of civilisation. Indeed the contrary is true. As civilisation becomes more rarefied, more dependent on watching instant history, more influenced by media personalities offering instant opinions of doubtful sincerity, there is an increasing delight in being primitive.

Yet you cannot live in a dream world, you cannot escape from reality; and the reality, always with us, was that the long costly struggle to put our plans into effect, the plans so hopefully made when we first came to Minack, were not receiving the material reward we had expected. Truth, we had discovered, was always changing.

Had I foreseen, for instance, years ago the array of equipment, glasshouses and bulbs by the ton we now possessed, I would have had no doubt that our future would be secure. That was the truth of the time. Certainly we still lived in the environment we loved, and every day, every moment of the day, we rejoiced in our good luck; but we never foresaw that conditions, fundamental to our livelihood, would change. We were like the majority. We had been living in a period when it was normal to believe that the world stood still. Our world at any rate. We therefore had believed that if one aimed at creating a happy situation which suited the present, the present would still be there when this happy situation had been attained. A naïve mistake to make. For when we had achieved our aim, the present as we had known it was no longer there. A tougher, vastly more expensive present was in its place.

Our experience during the past tomato season was an example. Tomatoes have been for years the breadwinner for growers, especially for those like ourselves who have a holiday trade on the doorstep, and no rail expenses in consequence. True it is a crop which requires an immense amount of tedious, hand labour to grow, and over a long period of time, but in normal circumstances the financial rewards were worth this trouble. It was certainly worth the trouble when Jeannie and I were planning our greenhouses. It seemed worth it, too, when later we decided to install automatic air heating, a heating method of oil-fired heaters with fans which blow the warm air through the greenhouse in polythene ductings. Indeed, at the time when we were poring over the catalogues first of the greenhouses and then of the heaters, we were sure that only lack of nerve on our part separated us from a summer income which would give us security. We needed nerve to raise capital. And when, after many adventures, the capital in each case was obtained, I said to Jeannie that the worst part of our endeavours was over. On both occasions I said this. First, after I had raised the money for the greenhouses; then again after I had raised the money for the heaters.

But I did not foresee, needless to say, the wage explosion and the consequent jump in our annual costs. Nothing unusual about this of course, though it does seem to me that market garden growers were affected more than most. Unlike farmers, for instance, growers are not cushioned by guaranteed prices. All their produce is sold on the open market and the prices obtained are dependent on supply and demand which in turn is controlled by the vagaries of the weather. A cold spell in summer means frustration for the lettuce grower; and we have sent splendid daffodils in January to Covent Garden, only to receive a poor price because the London area was snowbound.

Growers, therefore, are unable to raise their prices to balance their costs. Florists and greengrocers who receive the produce can do so, but growers can do nothing to counter the leap in oil charges, and freight, and fertilisers, and packaging, and all the necessities of growing. They also come under the control of the Agricultural Wages Board. When the Board decrees an increase in wages, farmers can be largely reimbursed when their annual Price Review is negotiated. But growers do not have this good fortune. Wage increases have to come out of their own pockets, irrespective of the financial state of their businesses. They are forced inevitably to cut down on staff, for only the cheerful, keen, experienced workers are worth-while retaining. These, in any case, will have wages above the legal minimum. Unfortunately, as the minimum wage rises, differentials are slowly erased; and yet the grower, however generous he may wish to be, cannot help any more. The decrees of the Agricultural Wages Board have seen to this. No wonder workers on the land become fewer and fewer every year.

This past tomato season was a bad one in any case. The June prices for tomatoes throughout the country (June being the month when growers with heated greenhouses rely on receiving high prices) were the lowest ever recorded for that time of year. Leaders of the tomato industry held an inquest to discover the cause; and they came to the conclusion that the great god efficiency had been up to his mischief again.

For growers, particularly the large growers, had set out to defeat costs by increasing their output of tomatoes. They had been aided by the army of research workers who operate in the background of the horticultural industry, both Government and private company research workers. These people have been so skilled in their researches, so persuasive in putting over their ideas to growers that the primary object of the grower to make money has been defeated. There are now too many greenhouses, too many skilled workers using precision methods of controlled environment growing, too many tomatoes. Efficiency had taken its toll again. Overproduction had killed the market. Growers, like their counterparts in other industries, were the victims.

So there I was sitting in the porch, invoices and price returns on the table, Jeannie now beside me, Nellie still above, probing our problems without coming to any conclusions, when the buzzer startled us with its alarm note. Startled Nellie also.

As I hurried down to the tank, I saw her flighting beautifully into the distance.

CHAPTER SEVEN

A week later the springs rose. I peered into the depths of the well, shining a torch on water that reached a jagged rock in the well wall; and the rock, I knew, was ten feet above the bottom. I now could dispense with my complicated arrangements. The automatic pump could be switched on. We were back on our personal mains.

'You mean I can use as much as I like?'

'Yes. No rationing.'

Down at Monty's Leap, the dribble of a stream had

widened and hastened. Car tyres, after crossing it, traced their damp marks for thirty yards instead of twenty. Stones no longer checked its flow, nor drooping weeds. The stream was gathering strength. Another week and it would be gushing into the reservoir, reaching the overflow gap, then into the undergrowth beyond, seeping down the valley until it found its course of previous winters, through brambles, beaten down bracken, wild mint, reeds, grasses, down, down, down, to the smooth rock of the cliff's face, and into the sea.

Winter had now become a companion. In the wood I found nests which I had not seen in summer. The bushes and trees were bare, and I suddenly discovered the tiny nest of the goldfinches who had haunted me in June and July with their bell-like chirruping, and darting red and gold. There it was in the hawthorn, just above me as I passed by Boris the drake's old hut, clusters of red berries now around it. A few yards away, within touching distance of the path, was a thrush's nest hidden in summer by the green leaves of the blackthorn; and cupped in the fork of another hawthorn was the nest of a chaffinch, and in the bank close to a magnolia was that of a robin and in the ivy that greedily climbed an ash-tree was a bundle of moss belonging to a wren, and in the branch of a willow were the dried sticks of a wood-pigeon's nest, and in one of the elms was the perfectly rounded hole of a green wood-pecker who never stayed to use it.

Winter unmasked summer. Summer had hidden the various things I had forgotten I had left in odd corners of the wood where I had left them year after year, each year intending to remove them until the year had gone and summer had returned, and I had done nothing. Discarded pieces of wire-netting now matted into the ground. Rusty sections of cloche frames. A battered, galvanised water trough for chickens. Jam jars now filled with compost from old leaves. The rotting roof of the chicken house, covered by ground ivy, in which Queen Mary, the Rhode Island Red who came with us from Mortlake, hatched her only chick. The bottom half of a broken hoe. A strand of barbed-wire. More wire-netting, and the stretch was still there against which Lama dashed hysterically when she was a wild kitten, trying to escape from the chicken run while I ponderously attempted to catch her. I touched her then, for the first time; and then away she ran, up a tree, on to the hut roof, a leap to a branch, down to the ground again, and out of sight. The wire-netting served no purpose now. We gave up the chickens long ago, and the hut, since Boris died, had only been used for the storing of fertilisers and other cumbersome goods. This winter, I said to myself, the wire-netting must be removed, so, too, the other tangible memories of the past. I must not be fooled by the lush greenery of another summer.

I walked further into the wood, scrambling over the barrier placed across a gap to stop the donkeys roaming further than their own donkey land. The big field to my left was theirs, and they were allowed into the remaining part of the wood because the trees were mostly elder, and they didn't fancy the bark of elder. But they were forbidden to enter the big meadow in front of me. Elms and hawthorns bordered three sides of it, and no elm or hawthorn was safe if the donkeys had a chance to reach it. The bark was a delicacy. That of the hawthorn they just gnawed, but they peeled off a strip of an elm, a softer bark, then gently ate it in the manner of someone enjoying asparagus. No tree could survive such attention, for as soon as the full circle of bark has been removed from a tree, however narrow it may be, the tree is certain to die.

The big meadow, the wood meadow, as it is called by us, was a jungle of undergrowth in summer when it came into our possession, and a bog in winter. We slashed the undergrowth away easily enough, but the bog tested our patience. Nothing could be grown in it until it had been drained, and yet it remained obstinately undrainable. We dug a ditch down the middle during the dry period of summer hoping that the water either side would drain into it when the springs rose. The ditch filled with water true enough, but the land still remained a bog. So the next summer we dug several ditches at angles to the main one, then waited for the winter to find out whether we had solved the problem. Once again we were disappointed. So the following summer we dug more ditches, until the meadow was littered with ditches. And when winter came we had the satisfaction of watching water in all of them merrily running to the main ditch which, with the gush of a small stream, took the water away from the meadow along a route leading to the

71

ditch from the lane, then to Monty's Leap, the reservoir and beyond. The next step was to lay pipes in all the ditches, shovel in the earth, taking care there was a tiny gap between each pipe to drain the land water, together with a few stones to prevent soil blocking the gap ... and then to plan the crop which would justify our persistence and our financial outlay.

We decided it would be an ideal meadow for bulbs, and it was just a question of what variety of daffodils we should choose. Unfortunately I was not feeling bold at the time. I was not in the mood to spend money, or take any kind of risk. Periodically in my life I have had this miserly attitude, a loss of nerve just when flamboyance was needed. Nor does this only concern money. I have found myself at some gathering where a show of personality might do me some good, or on some other occasion where it would be useful to give a good impression, and suddenly I am suffering from a load of inhibitions; and instead of being at ease, letting myself be myself, I talk too much, over-emphasise, make remarks that I later regret. Or I can be too serious, appearing to strain. In either case there is an inner-self watching detachedly, as if it were a tape recorder providing me with the evidence to contemplate upon afterwards. Usually my conclusion is that I lacked self-discipline to control my mood. Yet, although I accept that this may be true, I argue with myself that there are often extenuating circumstances. Dull people, for instance, people who look at you, glass in hand, but do not speak, bring out the worst in me. Intellectuals who belong to small, mutual admiring cliques, do so too. Also gun-happy gentry who rely on ancestors to justify their boisterousness. No need for self-blame when I fail with such people. But I would prefer, when I need confidence, that I kept my nerve. Just as I needed to keep my nerve when I had to decide what bulbs I should plant in the meadow.

Perhaps I was greedy. Or perhaps I was influenced by Jeannie who, in Scottish fashion, can be too generous at one moment and too careful at the next, in coming to the decision I did. I know now, in any case, that I regret the decision.

The previous year we had grown two tons of bulbs in the greenhouses. The venture had been partly provoked by the example of the Lincolnshire growers. If they could produce what amounted to *ersatz* spring daffodils under unnatural forced conditions and thereby capture a large part of the early market hitherto the preserve of Cornish and Scilly growers, why should we not try to have a pinch of the market? We would not force unnaturally however. We would not use heat, nor would the bulbs be pre-cooled. The daffodils would grow naturally except for the protection of the greenhouses against wind and excessive cold. Thus our daffodils, we felt, would qualify for that mystical attraction created by true spring daffodils.

Our pigmy effort against the big battalions had some success. We at any rate shared with them the prices prevailing in January; and we were certainly the only growers in our area who had daffodils to send away at that particular time of the year. Nevertheless the prices were not as high as we had expected, and in due course we decided we would not repeat the venture another year.

We still, however, had the bulbs and they all belonged to a variety called Golden Harvest, representing a capital investment of about £300. We had earned from them a little over £400, and so we had made a profit of £100. This was far too small a margin as far as we were concerned because, apart from the normal picking, bunching and sending away, there were the labour costs of planting them (the long greenhouse in front of the cottage had the bulbs in whalehide pots which had to be filled, planted and then transported) and then there were the labour costs of removing the bulbs after the daffodils had been harvested.

Yet if we could keep the bulbs, as we kept bulbs bought for the open fields, we would be earning a return on our investment for year after year; and it would seem obvious to do this. Forced bulbs, however, have to have time to recover; and the big growers with all the machines and facilities available to them will plant out their forced bulbs in the fields, lift them after a year, and then plant them again; and they reckon that in the third year the bulbs will be flowering again as normal. Some other growers, on the other hand, find the cost, time, and space involved not worth it; and they throw the bulbs away. We were advised by a master bulb grower to do this ourselves.

We did not agree with him. We considered our case

quite different. After all, we argued, we had not really *forced* our bulbs, not at any rate in the manner of the Lincolnshire growers. We had only provided protection during the growing period, protection which could be likened to an exceptionally warm and calm spring. We believed, therefore, that we could keep our bulbs, plant them again, and reap the harvest.

I had, on the other hand, doubts. The master bulb grower was so firm in his advice, so adamant that his opinion was the right one, that I would have been foolish not to doubt. Jeannie, however, thought otherwise ... the bulbs were a tangible asset, the master grower had no experience of our method of forcing, and we just could not afford to throw away £300 worth of bulbs. Obviously we couldn't. But irritatingly my doubts remained. Old growers, men who, over many years, have experienced the permutation of harvest results, have the knack of producing the right conclusions, however unpalatable they may be. And the man gave another reason to justify his advice. Golden Harvest, he said, was a tricky bulb.

Golden Harvest has been the rage in the markets for the past few years. It is a beautiful golden yellow daffodil with a light yellow perianth, and there is no doubt that it deserves to be greatly admired. But I see no reason why it mesmerises the salesmen in the markets and the florists to such an extent that equally beautiful daffodils like Joseph MacLeod and King Alfred are looked upon as inferior. The public, I am sure, cannot tell the difference between them. Yet sleepy-eyed florists disgorge from their vans at the markets in the early hours of each weekday morning, murmuring Golden Harvest to the waiting salesmen who of course are only too happy to oblige. Golden Harvest, therefore, has the power of a well publicised brand name; and growers naturally hasten to cater for the demand.

It happens, however, that the bulk of the Golden Harvest suffers in certain conditions from a fungus disease called basal rot. The disease causes a brown decay of the bulbs starting at the roots, and before long the bulb becomes a squishy mess beyond the hope of any recovery. Severe attacks, therefore, can decimate a meadow of bulbs within a couple of years, and those that are left will produce only short stemmed, weakly blooms, and it will be only a matter

74

of another year or two before they also disappear. And to add to the menace of basal rot, the fungus remains alive in the soil after the bulbs have rotted.

Nevertheless Golden Harvest thrives in ground it likes, and in such conditions shows no sign of disease. The only difficulty is to know which is the right ground and which is the wrong ground; and, at the time of our Golden Harvest, knowledge was incomplete because no one in our area had grown the bulbs. The knowledge is available today. I met the other day a doyen of daffodil growers who for many years has flower farmed the eastern slopes of Lamorna valley. He, too, had been axious to satisfy the demands of the sleepy-eyed florists. 'Golden Harvest?' he said to me, eyes under grey eyebrows giving the impression of contempt, 'they're no good for us. They're not happy on our cliffs.'

How right he was. How right, too, the master bulb grower who advised us to dispense with those greenhouse bulbs. We acted, ignoring his advice, ignoring the doubts I felt myself, by transporting the bulbs to the wood meadow; and planting them. We had even a sense of triumph when the planting was completed. Geoffrey in control, extra labour engaged; and the day when we looked upon the brown earth, sheltered all around by the elms and the hawthorn, was a day we felt was an achievement in our life here at Minack. It proved we were bold, and tenacious, and able to defy fuddy-duddy traditional caution like that of the master grower.

Inexperience, and the consequences, belong to any age. It is not exclusive to youth. But the youth has one great advantage because, in defeat, it is soothed by the notion that there are an everlasting number of years ahead in which to follow mistakes with victories. I still am soothed by this notion. I refuse to accept the fact, except when in a sad mood, that the options are becoming fewer.

This is just as well. There was an anaemic look about the Golden Harvest in the wood meadow from the moment they showed a few inches above the ground. They were in four-foot-wide beds, an eighteen-inch path between each bed, and they looked as if they required a good tonic. No, not even that, I realised, would help them. I watched them, pointing their weak, pale green foliage to the sky, a few accompanied by buds, and knew that we had made a major mistake. We had handed over a virgin meadow to a couple of tons of bulbs which hated the ground. Bulbs would rot there, spread their disease, and deny us the reward of the work and expense we had expended. Moreover I was aware that there was nothing we could do about it. Digging up bulbs was a far more laborious performance than planting them and we would never be able to spare the time to do so. Thus the decaying bulbs have remained there. Some still push up foliage, a few even produce daffodils. But I know now that I should have accepted the advice of the master grower. We were greedy. We did not want advice. Another option had gone.

So there I was staring at the wood meadow when I saw a movement in the far corner to the right, on the hedge built long ago of stones, now covered by grass, with an umbrella of hawthorn above it. First I thought the breeze was blowing a patch of tired bracken to and fro, then an instant later I saw quite clearly the head of a fox. I was not at first unduly surprised by the sight of it because foxes over the years have passed around Minack with nonchalant confidence. They would bolt, of course, if they came face to face with one of us, silently gliding away into the nearest undergrowth, but they never gave the impression of being on guard as they nosed around Minack. We were part of their landscape, and so they took us for granted. There were no dogs to chase them, no guns to frighten them. Only the donkeys to watch. Fred, looking for a diversion to help pass the time, would prick his ears when he saw a fox in his field, then advance towards it, first slowly, then at a canter, then at a gallop though the fox would long have disappeared over the hedge before he could reach it. Then Fred would stand balefully looking at the hedge, snorting.

But the fox I saw in the wood meadow was behaving in a most unusual manner. It was standing on the hedge, as if poised to jump down into the meadow; and swaying. Foxes are so quick in their movements, so decisive in carrying out what they want to do, that the sight of this fox behaving as if it was intoxicated was momentarily funny. Then suddenly it made up its mind to jump, and promptly sprawled flat on the ground.

I now started to walk quietly towards it. I could see it was a fine dog fox though not one I recognised as being recently in the neighbourhood. The coat was a paler bracken-red than usual, so, too, the head, though the sun shining upon it may have caused this impression. I was continuing to walk towards him, and was within twenty yards when he struggled to his feet, frightened obviously by my approach, and proceeded to run, not away from me but past me in the direction of that part of the wood which surrounded Boris's hut. He had not travelled far, not even out of the wood meadow, before he collapsed again. A moment later he was up, started to move forward, but only went round in a circle.

I thought at first he might have an injured leg, but the way he ran past me didn't suggest this. Clearly something was seriously wrong and, after seeing him desperately floundering around in a circle, then flop down again, it seemed likely that he was suffering from some kind of brain damage. He now lay not many yards from me with head stretched out on the soil, eyes nevertheless alert, and watching me.

I was sad enough not to move forward. Animals, like some human beings, prefer to be invalids on their own without people fussing; and I realised that whatever was wrong, there was nothing I could do to help. This fox was dying, so let him die on his own.

I thereupon retreated from where he was sprawled, stepped over the hedge where I first saw him, then pushed my way through some undergrowth, over another hedge and across a field to the lane which led down to the cottage. By taking this roundabout route, I had avoided advancing upon him, and so frightening him once again. I also had avoided any responsibilities that I might have had towards him, any second thoughts that it might have perhaps been my duty to be his executioner which, without a gun, could only have been clumsily achieved. Thus I returned to the cottage and Jeannie, unhappy of course, but consoled that I was letting nature take its course, letting a wild animal die a wild animal quite on its own.

Then suddenly half an hour later, I saw him at Monty's Leap, gulping from the stream. He was lying down as he did so.

'Jeannie!'

I was only at the corner of the cottage when I saw him, and I dashed back to tell her. She was hoovering the sitting-room carpet, and she didn't hear me above the whining hum of the machine.

'Jeannie!' I shouted.

The power was flicked off. There was silence.

'The fox!' I said urgently, 'the fox is down at the Leap!'

Immediately she came with me. The stone chippings would have sounded the alarm, had we moved quickly, and so we crept towards the Leap, taking advantage of stepping on the grass by the white seat and the verbena bush, then on the patch of grass opposite the old stable, and on the grass beside the lane until we were within a few yards of the fox. Poor soul, he had had his drink now and lay panting, a beautiful fox, helpless, years of roaming and hunting behind him; and being hunted.

'He's been poisoned,' said Jeannie softly.

'You can't know,' I said.

He moved then. He struggled to his feet, swayed, and turned his back on us; and tottered into the bushes of the little valley which took the stream from Monty's Leap. I suppose he was on his way back to his earth on the cliffs. I never saw him again. Later I searched the bushes and undergrowth of the valley, but there was no sign of him.

'He had been poisoned,' said Jeannie again.

'Why do you say that?'

'I just feel it.'

'Foxes have to die sometime. We just happened to be here to watch the end of a life. Young cub, mating fox, finish.'

'I still think he was poisoned.'

I had read about foxes being deliberately poisoned, but I had never heard of anyone in our area setting a bait of poison. But this fox could have come from afar. He could have been travelling over many miles, obeying this instinct which is strong in some foxes of going home when they are in trouble, going home to the earth where they were reared as young cubs. Or he may have picked up some poison by mistake. If he had been nosing about a farmyard, where rat poison had been laid, he might have done so. Strangely, Lama also was poisoned a week or two later.

We knew Lama was not well when she lost her purr; and we were immediately concerned one afternoon as we amused ourselves by courting her, by performing such delicate gestures as stroking her silky black head with a finger, when we were met by silence. Lama was always generous with her purrs, though she was equally generous with her squeaky growls if she considered we were being unduly attentive; and so when there was total silence, we were mildly alarmed.

'Did she eat her breakfast?'

'Only a little, now I come to think of it.'

'But she had it late, didn't she? I let her out before we listened to the news, and she was out for some time.'

'She came in about eleven.'

I am amused sometimes, in retrospect, by my tendency to be over-anxious. I am faced by a problem or an emergency, and promptly prepare for the worst so that I will not be shaken if it occurs. This attitude also means I am elated if my imaginary fears do not mature. My emotions, therefore, when trouble looms, are on a see-saw.

But if I was now showing over-anxiety, without any tangible reason as yet, it was because Lama was growing old; and I was haunted, always had been haunted, by the last weeks of Monty's life until the vet came and said he could do no more for him. This pain, universal though it is among those who love, remains unique to oneself. A personal agony which leaves an observer, however sympathetic, untouched; and only the cold never experience it.

Later that afternoon Lama showed the signs that our fears had a basis. She tried to be sick, and when we took her outside she slowly set off down the lane towards the stream, and when she reached it she crouched beside it drinking for minutes on end, just as Monty did when he was ill. Then she went into the grass and lay there although it had begun to rain.

That evening I went out and rang up the vet. Vets, I find, are so quick to respond to a call for help that sometimes I wish I was registered with a vet instead of a doctor. Our own vet, a Scotsman, was particularly zealous in this respect; and when he arrived in his large white car, from the moment in fact we saw it turn the corner in the lane beyond Monty's Leap, we felt reassured. He was merry, and sensible, and kind both to our anxious selves and to the patient whether a cat or a donkey. Thus when I rang up and found he had gone away for the night, and that both his partners were out on urgent missions, I was abruptly surprised. I had taken it so for granted that he would be out to see Lama within the hour instead of in the morning that I felt like someone who had suddenly been given the sack. Over-confidence, as always, had exacted its price.

Every now and then throughout the night I would wake up, my mind pleasantly clear of trouble for a few seconds, then blanketed with gloom as I remembered Lama. In reality I was remembering Monty. I was thinking of the years in between, from the time of Monty's death, Lama's strange arrival, and now; and I was angry, and puzzled and sad, that the years had run away so fast, and that I had so soon to feel again emotions I once thought would always be unique.

Lama was worse in the morning. She ignored the fish, a portion of her favourite ling, which Jeannie had poached for her; and drank instead a quantity of water. We were always amused by her manner of drinking water, because she would not have it in a saucer, as she would have milk. She insisted on drinking from an old-fashioned lemonade mug, of pink pottery decorated with flowers, which once was used by Jeannie's mother; and we had to keep it topped up because the water was out of her reach whenever it was a couple of inches from the rim of the mug. We topped it up a couple of times that morning, then carried her outside, put her down on the flower-bed close to the escallonia, and proceeded to watch her wobble to a patch of wet grass where she crouched as if the grass was cooling her tummy.

A few minutes later I heard the sound of a car. Our ears are tuned in to the grating of tyres on stone chippings and, if the weather is quiet, I can sometimes hear a car passing the farm buildings at the top of our lane; and then I follow the sound as it turns the bend until at last I see the bonnet as it comes into the final stretch towards Monty's Leap. The car I saw now, was white.

'He's arrived!'

The sight of the vet was enough to make us believe our fears were over. Without him saying a word, without any logical reason, we suddenly felt confident. The vet would never let Lama die. The vet had mysterious powers like those of a witch doctor; and we felt, now that he had arrived, as child-like as those who believed in witch doctors.

Came the usual questions.

'What were the first signs?'

'Has she cried?'

'Could she have come into contact with any poison?'

Jeannie and I, of course, had already conducted an inquest into Lama's immediate past. We could find no clue as a reason for her illness. We kept no poison on the premises. Some growers, on the other hand, stock pesticides and various forms of weed-killers because they insist it is necessary to do so. Such aids to profitable growing can be deadly dangerous; and I know one chemical product used for the sterilisation of bulbs which killed a grower's dog. A drop of the product had fallen into a puddle outside the house, and the dog drank from the puddle, and he died. Strange how the desire for efficiency blinds a person.

The vet sat on the sofa listening to our answers. Lama was on Jeannie's lap, held there, waiting for inspection. I was standing, puffing at my pipe.

'I wouldn't say she looks too bad,' said the vet, 'her coat's bright, so are her eyes. Think back once again. Can't you think of any clue at all? What about Geoffrey? Perhaps he has an idea.'

We had discussed the matter with Geoffrey. It is easy to talk to Geoffrey about animals and birds. We will waste time, for instance, during the day because we have seen an unusual migrant, or he may call to us that he has seen a hare, and we will leave whatever we are doing, and join him, watching. Pleasant intervals during the day's work are provided by such observations.

'Now, Lama,' said the vet, 'let's have a look at you.'

I left then. I had a sudden wish to talk to Geoffrey again, an instinct he might now remember some incident that would help. Clues are not always remembered immediately. Often they come into one's mind a long time after one has first sought them.

I found him having his croust, munching a slice of cake with his usual companions; a chaffinch, a pair of blue tits, a tom tit with one leg, waiting for crumbs to be thrown to them.

'We're still looking for clues,' I said; 'the vet seems to think she has picked up poison from somewhere.'

'I've been thinking,' he answered, 'I've got an idea.'

I listened as he told me his theory, then hurried back into the cottage.

'I think I have the answer!'

Lama had just received an injection, and she had wandered off across the carpet to beneath my desk, angry no doubt.

'I'm sure I have,' I said, then went on: 'When Geoffrey arrived yesterday morning, he found one of the dust-bins had been upset, lid off, and contents partly out. Half asleep he lifted it upright, and thought no more about it. He's suggesting that a fox must have tried to scavenge the contents during the night. Some of the contents had been there for nearly a week because dust-bin collecting day isn't till tomorrow. So Lama could have eaten something which had gone bad . . .'

'She couldn't be so greedy,' interrupted Jeannie.

'Well she was out long before Geoffrey arrived so she had plenty of time.'

'And you know how curious cats can be,' said the vet.

'Lama,' said Jeannie, addressing her across the room, 'I'm ashamed of you!'

Relief mingled with the shame. The injection, coupled with the medicine we gave her during the following twenty-four hours, changed our tottering Lama into a normal cat. Then came the happiest moment of all.

'Come here quickly,' Jeannie called to me, 'come and listen. Lama has found her purr!'

CHAPTER EIGHT

I saw Daisy, Lama's mother, the following morning in the stable meadow, slowly taking her usual route across it towards the cliff; a grey, compact little figure, seemingly unaware of the gale which was blowing up. She had some business in hand which she intended to complete; and the gale, and the salt which came with it, dampening her fur, sticky, was not going to deter her from fulfilling her secret task.

'Going to be rough,' I said to Geoffrey.

'Didn't hear the forecast.'

'Forecast said sunny periods and light winds.'

He laughed.

'Wrong again.'

Black clouds emptying their rain, were scurrying across the bay like upside-down mushrooms. At intervals the sun broke through, shining like a brilliant dagger on the sea. This was a sea that was glad of the turbulence to come, waves were slapping each other, leaving trails of foam in their wake, and watery pits; and above, yet so close that they seemed to be playing their own idea of Russian roulette, were the gulls. They dived at the waves, and swept through the spray; and settled, settled on the surging mass, bobbing spots defying the mountains which seemed at any moment to smother them. This was the beginning of the storm, the limbering up; and in an hour or so the gulls would have gone, gathered on sheltered rocks or inland fields, heads crouched in feathers, facing the wind, leaving the sea to rage.

'Better check that the greenhouses are all right,' I said.

I had greenhouse neurosis when they were first erected. I could not believe that they could withstand the gales which bashed them; and I would lie in bed listening to the roar outside, imagining the flying glass and the destruction of the crops inside, until I forced myself to get up, wrap myself in an oiler and, with a torch in my hand, set off to see the damage.

'Be careful,' Jeannie would say, 'do be careful.'

83

It was a long time before I rid myself of this neurosis, before I realised that greenhouses can be as tough as any building; and that although the glass may rattle like the sound of a thousand tin cans, making it a fearsome experience to be inside the greenhouse while the gale blew, it would need a whirlwind to destroy them.

But there was an occasion, the occasion of the worst gale in the Penzance area this century, when it seemed a whirlwind had anchored itself at Minack. The storm began the day before the famous Spring Show in Penzance; and Jane had come over from the Scillies where she worked at the Tresco Gardens, going there with her mother after she left working for us. She had brought with her a beautiful array of daffodils which she was entering for the Prince of Wales's Cup, the most coveted cup in the Show.

The weather was calm when she arrived, and she asked me whether I would mind her putting the daffodils in pails in the greenhouse, the long one in front of the cottage, because the blooms were backward and the warmth of the greenhouse would bring them out. That was a Tuesday afternoon, and entries for the Show had to be in their places by nine o'clock on Wednesday evening. Early on Wednesday morning the storm began; and by midday it was so fierce that the greenhouse was swaying like a drunken man, and the roof was leaping up and down. It appeared that any minute the whole structure would collapse ... and Jane's precious daffodils were still inside.

I told her that it was far too dangerous to open the door and fetch them. An open door would provide the funnel for the wind to rush in, and that would mean the end of the greenhouse for certain, and the risk was obvious that she might be lacerated by glass. Better, therefore, to leave the daffodils where they were.

Jane, however, had an ally in Jeannie. I was being too imaginative. My greenhouse neurosis had warped my judgement. It was absurd that I should dictate such orders just because I was scared of an open door. And so they plotted together that when I took our normal consignment of daffodils to catch the train at Penzance, they would act on their own. Just as well that they did. Jane won the coveted Prince of Wales's Cup, the youngest competitor ever to do so.

'All the vents are closed,' said Geoffrey after his inspection, 'and I've tried the doors.'

There was nothing in the greenhouse at the time. The tomato plants had been pulled up during October and the process of sterilising the soil set in motion. We never sterilised by steam, partly because of the initial expense of buying the equipment, mainly because of the lack of water at the time we had to do the steaming. We used a chemical instead, a powder which was rotovated into the soil. The soil was then lightly watered so that the fumes let off by the powder were sealed in the earth; and then for six weeks the greenhouses were kept closed while the germ and fungus destruction took place. No chance, therefore, to grow a winter crop; and so, whether we liked it or not, we had to depend on tomatoes to warrant the existence of the greenhouses. The past season's poor prices had to be forgotten. Optimism had to be drawn upon once again, and the plans laid for next summer.

'I've ordered the Maascross,' I said to Geoffrey.

I had been late in ordering the plants. Here it was the beginning of December, and the seeds had to be sown by the middle of the month. Sometimes we had considered growing our own plants, but we always checked from doing so because we realised that at the time they would need most attention, pricking out and so on, we would be immersed in the daffodil season; and the daffodils left us no time to spare. Thus at first I used to have the plants from the Land Settlement Association at Newent in Gloucestershire; and they were brought in a vast van which, on one occasion, half toppled over into the ditch as it came down our narrow lane. They were excellent plants but became too expensive; and now we have them from a Cornish grower at Truro called Hitchens who brings them to us early in March, a foot high, for planting out. As for the reason why we have the variety Maascross, the answer is that it likes our soil. We have tried others such as Eurocross, Moneymaker, Ailsa Craig, but none grows so well as does Maascross. The tomatoes also have a very fine flavour although this factor is now considered unimportant. Bulk sellers of tomatoes require only tomatoes of uniform shape. They must all be of exactly the same size. The prepack mentality demands this. It does not demand any flavour. But in Cornwall during the holiday season, old-fashioned pleasures are enjoyed again; and our tomatoes with the slogan, 'Tomatoes Grown for Flavour', stamped on the side of the containers, are always in demand.

The rain was now falling on Minack; and the sound of it as it swept through the trees, and the sound of the gale pausing, rushing, shouting as if in argument, produced in me a sudden sense of exultation. I left Geoffrey in the hut which was his office, the hut where we first bunched daffodils, where I constantly knocked my head against the cross-bar in the middle, sometimes cutting it, until Jane and Shelagh covered the bar with foam rubber . . . and went outside into the storm. I glanced at the primitive building which acts as a garage, and noticed Nellie sheltering, perched on one of the rocks jutting out of the bank which serves as one side of the building. Nellie was safe there, and comfortable, and happy so it seemed. Why therefore did she always fly away when dusk fell? And where? I was to find out one day, yet even the answer puzzled me.

I went out and braced myself against the rain and the gale, and strode to the gate of the stable meadow, a chewed, wooden gate, made so by the donkeys when they were bored by the absence of attention; and I passed through the gate, passed the donkeys themselves as they stood, bottoms to the hedge, heads down, tolerating the storm with a dopey attitude of patience. Yet the barn door was open for them. They had only to move there and be out of the wind and the rain, but no. They desired to indulge in donkey masochism. They preferred to maintain the donkey tradition that they were a persecuted race.

On I went along the path, across Fred's field, down to the little gate at the top of the cliff, down the steps, down through the pocket meadows, past the palm tree which I planted when my mother died, through the narrow gap between two hedges of blackthorn and into the bottom daffodil meadow of all, then down again to the point where the grass ended and the grey rocks began. Here was my journey's end. Here I stood with the grandeur of a Cornish sea just below me, watching it foaming the rocks where we lazed on summer days, watching the great waves mounting their assault, coming nearer and nearer, and growing, and the tops curving and sharpening so that for a split second the tops resembled a knife's edge before they thundered down on the rocks which halted them. This was a scene which belonged to immortality. I was seeing the same waves, hearing the same roar, wet with the same spray, nothing had changed throughout the centuries. This was the universe. This was the back-drop to all history, to all conflicts between nations or individuals, to impatient ambitions, to the passing fashions of each age, to the vanity of man. This was continuity which some ignore, some deride; and in which some find comfort. Man's conceit as he overpopulates, drowns the countryside in concrete, pollutes the sky and the rivers, will surely wither. One day he will learn the universe is master.

A seal was in the teaspoon of a bay to my left, the tiny bay where once Jeannie and I tried to solve our fish supply by having a trammel net stretching across from a galvanised ring cemented in a rock to a buoy forty yards out. The trammel net had two ropes, one to pull out the net, one to pull it in; and for a few weeks we had much excitement as we harvested the fish. Most were wrasse and uneatable, but we caught some pollack, a mackerel or two, and even a conger-eel. But a gale came and took away our net; and instead of cheap fish, we realised we had the most expensive fish we have ever eaten. One day, perhaps, we will try again; for it is always a minor triumph if one corrects a past mistake.

I was not surprised by the sight of the seal, for I had seen one there before in a storm. On that occasion I first thought it was a piece of wood, then it might be the body of a drowned person, then I realised it was a seal which seemed to be relishing in its defiance of the storm. So now. This seal I was watching, insolently awaited the curving waves; and when they crashed down on the rocks, they appeared to crash down on him, so close was he himself to the rocks. Then the waves, splintering their white, rushing froth into crevices and high points which were dry except in the great storms, which gulls themselves normally believed to be high ground, reluctantly receded and I saw the seal again, head and whiskers above water, a grey knowing face, amused that he had defeated, as he always would defeat, the rage of a storm.

Our coast is not usually seal country. I have never, for

instance, seen a seal basking on a rock, nor have I ever seen more than one seal at a time. Seals prefer the north coast, places like the island of rocks called The Carracks near St Ives, or Hell's Mouth between Hayle and Portreath, or St Agnes where there is a seal sanctuary soon to move to Perranporth. But there is another stretch of the coast 'nearer to us, a stretch we sometimes walk and which is one of the most beautiful walks in the world, where a seal once gave us a magical experience.

We had left the car at Porthgwarra, a hamlet at the end of a valley with a slipway between rugged rocks leading to sand and the sea. It is the last hamlet on the south coast of Cornwall, and it lies sheltered from the westerlies by the massive promontory of Gwennap Head, on the fierce cliffs on which marine commandos train to climb. Tol Pedn coastguard station stands at the top, a box of a building manned day and night, where every passing vessel is recorded, where the *Torrey Canyon* was observed as she sailed towards the Seven Stones reef in the distance.

Below the station are the coastguard dwellings, solid homes huddled together, resembling a fort; and they edge a vast area of barren land, barren except for the heathery ling and stunted gorse which covers it like a giant cushion. Here pause the migrant birds; and here, from time to time, we have flushed a quail, and seen a grey shrike, small to be so fierce, and watched wheatears bobbing their tails, displaying their white rumps, listened to the rattle of grasshopper warblers without any sign of them, observed cuckoos scouting for rock pipit nests; and always, of course, there are the swallows, resting on the telephone lines running down the valley after arrival, resting again before departure. Reasonable enough that this is a place for birdwatchers.

But there are seals, too, to watch. The coastal path leads away from the coastguard dwellings, around the rim of Porth Loe Cove, and upwards, until it levels out on the edge of the cliff high above the sea. From here, on clear days, you can see the shadowy outline of the Scilly Islands; and, in the morning, you will see the white speck of the *Scillonian* on the way there from the mainland, passing the lonely Wolf Rock lighthouse where a keeper was swept away not long ago as he fished from its base. On your right, if you are facing the sea, and four miles away, is the Longship lighthouse, most photographed lighthouse in Britain; and, as if adjoining it though there is a mile of sea in between, is the tourist mecca of Land's End. It is fashionable to condemn the ugliness of this mecca, but I do not find it as ugly as its reputation. There are only five shops, all low-roofed, and the hotel with its magnificent views has none of the offensive, utility coldness of modern hotel buildings. There is the car park, of course, and the crush of people in summer, disgorging from coaches, wearing funny hats; but go there in spring, and autumn, and winter, and you will experience the loneliness of the place. It is at the village of Sennen, a mile away, where man flaunts his ability to destroy beauty; for here is a site of permanent, crude caravans, so situated that, from afar, the lovely centuries old-church seems to be surrounded by them. Nor has any satisfactory attempt been made, although the site has been there for many years, to screen it within a shelter of trees. It remains, unashamed, a monument to man's vandalism.

Below Tol Pedn coastguard station are the rocks where seals gather, and it is at the point on the coastal path above Porth Loe Cove that you can observe them. There is nothing secretive about them, and we have often watched them slithering on and off the rocks, playing games with each other, sometimes immobile, ruminating, two or three grey-black seals, perhaps a couple which are creamy-coloured. Sometimes, also, we have heard them singing, but their sound was raucous compared to the song of the seal which provided us with the magical experience.

We were following our usual route, past Folly Cove, along Ardensaweth Cliff, aiming for Nanjizal Bay. It is a little bay and in some summers it has a beach of sand; in others, if the weather has been stormy, it has a beach of boulders. We never, as it happens, go down to the beach ourselves, but it serves as a terminal. We reach the cliff above it, look down, remark upon its state, then return the way we have come.

On this occasion we had reached a steep dip in the walk, between Ardensaweth Cliff and Nanjizal Bay, which opens on another bay called Pendower Coves. Down you then walk into the narrow valley, then across a little stream where wild cotton grows alongside in summer; and then up the other steep track towards Carn Les Boel, and Nanjizal. It is pleasant on such a walk to have no human being in sight; and it is remarkable how often such freedom from distraction is obtained. In solitude one becomes part of the grandeur of the scenery, and involved in its rugged past. One does not want to be reminded of today. One wishes to enjoy illogical emotions, like the irrational awareness that one has been there before, and that one's spirit will always be there. Thus, when Jeannie and I see somebody on the horizon coming towards us, we plan avoiding action. Others, we have found, take similar action if they see us. A local lady, a dedicated lover of this walk for many years, stopped me in Penzance one day. 'I hope,' she said, 'you don't take it personally when I hide from you on the Porthgwarra walk.' 'Of course not,' I said, 'while you are hiding behind one rock, we are hiding behind another.'

We had reached the dip, Jeannie and I, had almost reached the stream, when we heard from across the still water a sound like a flute being played.

'Listen,' I said, 'a seal is singing.'

No movement. No speech between us. It was a sighing, ethereal sound; and it was coming from inside a great cave that burrows into the cliffs.

'Mary Rose,' said Jeannie, 'it is like the song of the fairies in Mary Rose.'

I left the other seal, the seal in our teaspoon of a bay, and started back up the cliff. I did not hurry. I am by inclination a stroller, not a walker; and I have often irritated Jeannie by my dawdling. I prefer to pause, and look around, and contemplate. Jeannie likes to reach her destination. I prefer to delay doing so . . . even in a storm.

I paused, therefore, by the palm tree, sheltering below its sword-shaped leaves, the trunk swaying, the leaves cackling as the gale rushed by; and I stood facing the gale and the sea, spray mingling with the rain on my face, elated by this fury of nature, clouds lowering, and the roar so loud that no one would have heard me had I shouted across the meadow. I saw a fishing boat heading for Newlyn, one of the Stevenson trawler fleet I realised; and then another, a smaller one; and closer inshore there was a French crabber with an all white hull, and as it heaved between the waves, then momentarily riding one like a surfer, I could see the

90

crew in the stern, matchsticks of bright orange-red. Bigger vessels would be coming soon; and almost immediately I caught sight in the dropping visibility of the outline of a small coaster, foreign no doubt, whose captain had decided that the shelter of inner Mount's Bay was a wiser place to be than rounding the corner of Land's End. By nightfall, I was sure, there would be several boats riding at anchor within sight of Penzance's promenade.

I moved from the palm tree and went up the cliff, pausing again just before I reached the little gate which led to Fred's field. I was staring downwards now, down at the turbulence of the sea, down at the fishing boats and the French crabber, down at the coaster and another one which had just come into view. And down, I realised, at my past.

For this cliff was the lure which led us away from our London lives; and on that day, sickle and scythe in our hands, when we began to slash order into the cliff, opening up again long-forgotten meadows and creating new ones, we truly believed that the world stood still. Machines? Horticultural industrialisation? We were so naïve that we never considered such things would interfere with our future, never considered the possibility of man-made over-production. Only the elements, we thought, would be our enemy; and when in due course we endured gales which pulverised our crops, or a sudden frost which destroyed six months' income in a night, we were comforted by the knowledge that nature had been the architect of our defeat, not man. Nature represented freedom, and could be forgiven; man, in contrast, offered chains, and more chains. Man's mistake is to believe that freedom is orderly.

Hence we relished the earthy philosophy of our neighbours and of those who helped us. Their words were shouts of defiance against the trends of civilisation.

'I've lost my waistcoat, boy,' said a farmer as he surveyed a field of potatoes, haulms blackened by a gale. 'And where am I going to find my waistcoat again? Why, right here . . . next year!'

We had helping us, during our beginning, a tall, lean, eccentric Cornishman called Tommy Williams who lived alone in a caravan not far away. He was middle-aged, believed women a nuisance, would suddenly burst into hymn singing as he was digging a meadow, ate only out of tins, and prided himself on being a collector of *objets d'art*. These were of a varied nature. I remember him arriving one Monday morning with the news that on the previous Saturday in Penzance he had bought a Rembrandt. On another occasion he announced that he had discovered in a junkshop a Stradivarius violin. He spoke of his finds in such authoritative fashion that I never dared question their genuineness; and for weeks afterwards, as I pursued some earthy task in his company, I would have to listen to his future plans for them. The Rembrandt, I remember, was understandably scheduled for Christies. The Stradivarius, on the other hand, was to be kept.

'I've always had a mind to play the violin,' he explained to me.

Tommy had many qualities. He was adept at moving rocks, and there were many rocks at the time to move. He would often work overtime, then refuse any pay for it. He was a good shoveller, and it was he who taught me to use the long-handled Cornish shovel. And he was constantly presenting me with ingenious ideas, few of which proved practical. Once, for instance, during a rainy period which was causing him to be behindhand in the task of turning ground for the coming potato season, he proposed that I should buy him a tent. He would turn the ground while sheltering in the tent. A praiseworthy idea, no doubt, but unfortunately he had not taken into account the wind which came with the rain.

But as I stood, looking down at the meadows, looking down at the sea pounding the rocks, looking down at the boats making for the shelter of Newlyn, I could see Tommy again. There he was in that meadow to the right, having discovered a tiny spring, and already a grandiose plan was forming in his mind. He would harness this spring, build a dam, build a reservoir . . . henceforth there would be no water problems on the cliff. No drought would ever again spoil a potato crop. More important still he would have the edge on others in the neighbourhood, men with whom he had grown up, men he had worked for . . . *their* potatoes would be like pebbles. Only Minack cliff potatoes would be large. Alas, the spring died when summer came.

Tommy wearing a Panama hat in summer, a peak cap in winter. Once I found him on his knees groping in the grass around the edge of a meadow, and I asked him what he was doing.

'An unusual insect. A very unusual insect. I'm trying to catch it.'

And there were other times when I would sit beside him in one of the meadows of the cliff, listening to comical stories which I had no means of knowing whether they were true. I was then still a Londoner. I was learning to be a countryman.

'Chickens,' he would say, 'fly up into a tree when they sense a fox is about ... so what does the fox do? He will walk round and round the tree, for half an hour or more, and the chicken will be watching him until it becomes dizzy and falls to the ground.'

'Dirty animals, foxes,' he would explain, 'badgers won't have anything to do with them ... badgers are real house-proud. But there's one thing I can say in favour of foxes. They can't stand fleas. If a fox has fleas he will go looking for a stream or a pond, pull a tuft of hair from his coat, then stand in the water still holding the tuft in his mouth. He will go on standing until the fleas, to escape drowning, have all collected on the tuft. Then he lets it go.'

I slowed down with Tommy. I was like a schoolboy who, at a formative time, has the luck to have a teacher who reflects, but with experience, the boy's own feelings. I became aware of small pleasures. I learnt that to enjoy such pleasures I had to have patience. They are not revealed to those who hurry. I learnt, and years later this lesson is much sharper, that many of us are like puddings in our reaction towards the senses.

For this is a visual age. Our eyes are satiated by pictures which capture our admiration, or our weakness for gaping, but which do not capture our involvement. We travel the world and space in our armchairs, marvelling at the photography as we land on the moon, explore the Nile, study land-crabs on some island in the Indian ocean, watch a soldier on guard against a sniper's bullet at a modern city's street corner, climb the vertical face of a mountain, participate in an Asian flood disaster, observe white horses galloping in the Camargue, round the Horn in a boat too small for survival to be expected. Every evening of our lives we seem to be acting as observers. A new generation is growing up which even considers this observer way of life as normal. These people watch a storm, and do not feel the wind and the rain. They are in a pine wood and do not smell the pines. They look at danger but do not experience it. Emotion is missing. Only the eyes count. Only curiosity is satisfied.

But how can anyone be blamed for reacting like this? Few people have the chance to live life slowly, to live amidst beautiful surroundings. You have to have luck to be able to do so. You have to have luck to avoid living life second-hand. You have to have luck to be able to enjoy the small pleasures.

Small pleasures like the spread of a red admiral butterfly on an ivy leaf in autumn. A green woodpecker with crimson head, clasped to the trunk of a bare tree. Golden plover in a ploughed field on a December afternoon. Red berries of hawthorn. Woodsmoke curling away from your own hearth. Piping of a snipe as it zig-zags like a flying firecracker away from you, safe because you have no gun. A December primrose, and you bend down, and the frail scent touches you, turning away your worldly cynicism. The daffodil spikes showing in the meadows where the donkeys enjoy their winter roaming. Time now to ban them because their hooves will crush the spikes. Small excitements . . . like the heron who slowly dropped into our reservoir one morning, floating down with legs hanging, like the wheels of an aircraft. I hurried to tell Jeannie, hiding the sound of my footsteps by walking where possible on grass. But the gull on the roof had also seen the heron, and was screeching, urging other gulls to screech too, until the heron floated up again from the reservoir, sedately climbing into the sky, ignoring the common people who were bawling at him.

Jeannie once imagined a joke method of measuring happiness. She invented in her mind an instrument called a happometer, designed on the same principle as a car milometer or a walker's pedometer, except that it was operated manually. Her idea was to measure each moment of happiness during the day by pressing a button on this happometer; a touch for a flash of happiness, a long touch for some out of the ordinary happiness. Thus a business tycoon might push long and hard at the button after a successful takeover bid, a politician perform the same after rousing an audience to hail a policy which gives him some personal kudos, and Jeannie would celebrate in the same fashion because, perhaps, she had been thrilled by the dying evening light on winter bracken, the sea beyond; or she had experienced delight in some small pleasure like an unsolicited purr from Lama. Her use of the happometer, therefore, displayed no practical appreciation of the sensible world we live in. Yet her reactions were of the kind which can bring another dimension to living ... if we are patient, cease sometimes to be community minded, if we allow emotion occasionally to govern us, instead of intellect. Then occur moments which can take us away from conventional reality. Aloneness, we discover, can be more rewarding than being part of a herd.

It was time to go. The storm had ended its skirmishing, ended its first flush of magnificence, and now had begun the hours of solid battering. There would be no work to do outdoors today. Geoffrey could saw logs, I thought, but first we had better go together to have a look at the ditch that ran down the hill beside the lane. A blockage, and the water would gush over into the lane itself, turning it into a river-bed, seering still further the already rough surface. Many occasions I had forgotten to check the ditch in time. And then I would take the donkeys into the stable whether they wanted to go or not. They themselves would be prepared to stand bottoms to a hedge throughout the storm, but I could not bear the lugubrious sight of them. So much more comforting as I sat indoors before the fire, to know that the donkeys were away from the gale and the rain.

I turned to go up the few steps and through the little gate to the big field when suddenly I had a feeling that I was being watched. A second later I saw Daisy, ten yards away, crouched at the foot of a bank of brambles.

'Daisy!' I called out, 'this is a mad place for you to be in such weather.'

She stared back at me, and I am sure she was thinking to herself that I, too, was mad. I had a home to go to where I could be dry and warm, so why wasn't I there? She belonged to the storms. She had been a part of them all her life, and she knew how to cope with them. She had hiding places, clefts in rocks, and earthy corners, an umbrella of undergrowth overhead. Yet why was she watching me? She had always had this habit of watching, watching, watching. It seemed she wanted to involve herself with us but on the terms of her complete independence.

'Daisy,' I said, 'you are a funny cat the way you never ask for anything.'

Just a stare.

'And the way you never come within touching distance.'

Still a stare.

'Yet you behave as if you belong here. I wonder what goes on in that mind of yours.'

I left her where she was, not a sign of her wishing to come with me.

But she did come to us in the end. We touched her too.

CHAPTER NINE

We had acquired during the summer a squirrel attitude towards the winter. We had decided to hoard. We aimed to create a supply situation whereby we could withstand a siege.

A caller first set me on this policy. We have many callers during the course of a year, and we learn much from them. One caller advised me to buy shares in the company he worked for because there was soon to be a takeover bid. The bid took place, the shares shot up, and I was left with a groan: 'Why didn't I take his advice?' Another caller was an expert at field mushroom growing, something which Jeannie had always wanted to do, and promised he would send us a bagful of the spawn at the appropriate time of the year. It never arrived, and this has left Jeannie with another groan: 'All Minack would now be littered with mushrooms if he had remembered to send it.' Other callers have been more productive. From university students one learns that the basic aspirations of youth are no different from one's own, years later in age. From others one discovers that solitude, in contrast to loneliness, is still considered by the sensitive to be a prize. Again and again one marvels at the courage that is shown by the sick and blind, and those that are victims of bad luck or great sadness; and always, surprisingly perhaps, one is aware of the happiness that most people have in each other's company.

There was, however, this caller, who put forward to us a very practical idea. She had brought her daughter to Minack to meet the donkeys; and while the girl was feeding Penny and Fred with the carrots she had brought, the mother began extolling to us the virtues of the deep freeze she had at home. I listened sceptically. I had heard other stories which did not measure up to her enthusiasm; and these stories had substantiated my instinctive distrust towards the machine, if a deep freeze can be called a machine. One friend described a luncheon party at which Dover sole from a deep freeze had been served with unfortunate results. Another described how, because of the box-like design of a deep freeze, one never reaches the frozen food stacked at the bottom. Another that meat from a deep freeze was always tough. There were also the usual accounts of frozen food possessing no flavour. Indeed, as far as I was concerned, frozen food was synonymous with tastelessness.

Our visitor now proceeded to correct this attitude of mine and, further, also proceeded to enlighten Jeannie as to the time and expense which she would be able to save if we possessed a deep freeze. It was at this moment that I realised that deep freeze addicts, like rally drivers, race-goers, football fans, and everyone else who is devoted to some particular hobby, are apt to overwhelm their listeners with their technical enthusiasm. Our visitor certainly overwhelmed me. She departed with her daughter leaving me in a haze; and I only wish I could have met her again to tell her that when I came out of the haze, Jeannie and I had become deep freeze addicts ourselves.

Thus when now I meet someone whom I believe would benefit from a deep freeze I immediately launch into the attack, ignoring the fact that it is none of my business.

'A deep freeze will change your life,' I cry, 'and the money you'll save will be enormous. Fish and meat wholesale! All those peas and runner beans which run to seed in your vegetable garden because there are too many to eat when they are ready . . . all these will be in the deep freeze. Then the fruit! Raspberries, strawberries and blackberries. And the ready cooked dishes like steak and kidney pie, and goulashes, and stews . . . Jeannie prepares a dozen at a time, a dozen meals which only have to be warmed up!'

At this stage, in true addict fashion, my enthusiasm has grown out of hand. I have adopted a missionary zeal. I am like a hot gospeller wishing to spread the good news that I have seen the light. My listener looks apprehensive. My listener, especially if he scarcely knows me, wonders how he can change the subject But I relentlessly continue to drive my points home . . .

This behaviour of mine, however, has often been prompted by the desire to find a subject of conversation. I am thrust into the company of someone with whom I seem to have little in common, find my sentences reaching nowhere, and so resort to the deep freeze. Thus I sometimes use the deep freeze as a ploy; and recently I used it as a ploy of minor revenge against a charming lady whom I sat next to at a luncheon party. This lady, as soon as she had sat down, and having no clue to my past or present, straight away shot this question at me.

'What *practical* things do you do?' she demanded.

I have learnt since, that this is a familiar question at diplomatic gatherings. It is a question that helps to bring a diplomat alive. You are in a crowded room, champagne glass in your hand, saddled with a diplomat from some new country you have never heard of, and you hurtle at him the question: 'What *practical* things do you do?' The answer is sure to be informative. It will give you an idea of the part of the world he comes from. He will be flattered that you are interested in such a personal way; and his attention will be held long enough for you to catch the eye of a friend who will come and rescue you.

I, however, failed to satisfy my luncheon companion with my answer. She had, in fact, taken me so much by surprise that my answer was a garbled sentence.

'Well, er . . .' I said, 'well, I write. I write books.'

This clearly did not fit in with diplomatic form. She had no notion of what books I had written, and my answer had given her no clue. So she repeated the question, this time with even greater emphasis on the word *practical*.

At this point I caught sight of Jeannie looking at me across the table with amusement. She had guessed I was having difficulties. I was in even greater difficulties a minute or two later.

My companion, casting a charming glance around the table, but still managing to make it seem she was waiting expectantly for my answer, now received an answer which even surprised myself.

'I also cook,' I said.

This indeed was a remark of desperation. It was certainly a foolish remark. It was not original. Had I been a diplomat from an undeveloped country it would have had no chance of bringing a light to the eye of a sophisticated official of the United Nations. There would have been no chance of a quietly taken note: 'Met an intelligent chap at the Mauretania party tonight. Must see what we can do for this new country of his.' No positive thought would come out of a remark like mine. I would have failed my new country. What United Nations official could possibly be interested in my cooking?

Clearly I was off balance. My companion had succeeded in unnerving me; and I believe the reason lay in the sweeping fashion that people, accustomed to meeting countless strangers, are sometimes inclined to appear superior as a means of personal defence. They cannot know everyone with affection, even though they might like to; and so they gush on with words that have no meaning. Or ask questions out of habit. As my delightful luncheon companion proceeded to do.

'Cook?' she said, toying with her smoked salmon, 'that's practical ...' I thought at this moment that I had successfully dealt with the situation when she added: 'And *what* do you cook?'

This, of course, added to my confusion. I would have liked to have replied: 'Bangers!' ... and left it at that. But my companion had succeeded in imposing her personality upon me; and I was now a little frightened of her. My muddled mind even wanted to impress her; and so a second or so afterwards I heard myself murmuring: 'I cook special dishes ... very special dishes.' Just as if I was Robert Carrier.

It was a disastrous moment. My companion suddenly turned her full attention upon me, as if at last she considered I was a person of consequence.

'Special dishes?' she exclaimed, her voice throatily charming. '*Do* tell me ... *what* special dishes do you cook?'

She had floored me, and I threw in my towel. I didn't even attempt a reply. I just looked at her and asked:

'Have you a deep freeze?'

Then launched my counter-attack.

I will now, however, quell my over-enthusiasm. I want to be serious about our deep freeze, and explain how its installation has influenced our daily lives. The daily life of Lama, for instance.

Lama turns up her nose at normal cat foods. She may consume the first spoonful of a newly opened tin, but that is enough. She walks away with her tail in the air if we offer her a second. Hence we have always tried to keep her supplied with fresh food; and when this has run out, so anxious have we been to please her that we have broken away from our work to drive the five miles to Newlyn and the butcher or the fishmonger. Not any longer. Not any longer are we faced by a bare larder, not any longer do we have to waste petrol and time catering for a cat. Nor do we have to pay the high prices of winter when storms have kept the fishing boats in harbour. At the end of September we bought 70 lbs of ling, a favourite Lama fish, at a glut price of ten new pence a pound, each pound in a polythene packet of its own; and for a change of diet packets of minced beef await to delight her.

Penny and Fred, on the other hand, gain no benefit at all. Nothing on their diet needs a deep freeze. Their carrots are stored in net bags, hay in bales, and the pony pellets for which they have a passion, in bags. But the gulls benefit in a roundabout way.

There are the five regulars. A pair who fly up from the Lamorna direction, a pair who come from our own rocks; and Philip, who usually comes when the others are absent. Philip is a sedate old boy, a contemplative gull, and he never shouts for his dinner. The others, however, bawl their heads off, and there has been many a time when I have been compelled to go out and bawl back at them: 'Shut up! Shut up!'

Earlier gulls of ours like old Hubert, Squeaker, Knocker, and Peter, certainly were raucous at times but never were they so persistently noisy as the present four. But they may have a reason.

These gulls used to have Jeannie's home-made wholemeal bread; but only Philip has it now as a kind of old age pension. The reason is that Jeannie found she was spending more time baking bread for the gulls than she was for ourselves, and so she rightly said the gulls would have to put up with shop bread. Unfortunately, up to this time, the gulls had shown no interest in shop bread. We had thrown pieces up on the roof but after a peck or two they had left the jackdaws to swoop on the roof and carry the pieces away. Therefore it took a while for the gulls to realise that they were living under a new regime; and that they were now obliged to eat the bread consumed by the majority of people in this country.

They did, of course, have changes of diet. Odd bits of

101

fat, fish skin, discarded pastry; and there were the occasions when we had eggs and bacon for breakfast. All of them seemed to know what we were having within a few minutes of the bacon sizzling in the frying-pan. They were after the rinds; and we tried to distribute them fairly, though we were always biased towards Philip. He was so much the more intelligent. Hence, on these occasions, he refused as always to mix with the others on the roof, but stood instead on a grey rock at the edge of the donkey field just above the cottage. Sometimes the donkeys were within nose touching distance of him; and when we threw a rind at him, he would catch it in his beak, then sail away into the sky, leaving the donkeys watching him.

The others, the noisy ones, have their shop bread in slices from packets; and before the arrival of the deep freeze the contents of these packets used quickly to go mouldy. Thus, although the gulls may desire Jeannie's bread, they at least now have their shop bread fresh.

Now this bread of Jeannie's is of remarkable quality. It *tastes* of bread; and I quite understand why the gulls preferred it to any other. It puzzles me sometimes why the bakery trade cannot offer bread of similar quality. They have the flour. They have the knowledge. But it seems the bakery trade has suffered more than most for the sake of efficiency and the cutting down of costs. Brilliant methods have been devised to produce their products with economy but without flavour; and a generation has grown up which expects no better.

When I was a Billy Bunter schoolboy I revelled in doughnuts, chocolate eclairs, Bourbon chocolate biscuits, various cream buns, and particularly a marvellous walnut cake with soft powdery icing on the top. But doughnuts do not taste like doughnuts any more, nor eclairs like eclairs, nor Bourbon biscuits like Bourbon biscuits; and the biggest disappointment of all is the walnut cake. It still has the same proprietary brand name as the cake with which my mother consoled me before my return after the holidays to school, a last present which she thrust into my hands while I wondered how much of it I would have to share with my schoolboy companions. Then it was a marvellous cake. Today the contents of the cake have the texture of froth. Mass production has ruined my schoolboy cake.

102

Jeannie's bread, of course, also now goes into the deep freeze. This is of special help to her because the bread requires an effort to make, even a manual effort, and she now can bake twice as much at a time. She used to bake four pounds a week, but by the end of the week the last loaf, though not stale, had certainly lost its newness. Now she wraps each loaf in a polythene bag, puts it in the deep freeze, and by the end of a fortnight the last loaf is as new as the first. Nor does a loaf take long to thaw out. A loaf brought from the deep freeze after breakfast is ready by lunchtime. And here is the recipe she uses. It is an old one and comes from her mother's family.

Out of three pounds of wholemeal flour and three tea-spoonfuls of dried yeast, you can make four one-pound loaves. While the yeast is dissolving in a cup of warm water, you mix half the flour, a tablespoonful of brown sugar and one of coarse salt in a warmed basin. To this you add about one and a half pints of warm water mixing it all into a batter; then add the dissolved yeast, mix it in, and leave in a warm place for fifteen minutes or so. The rest of the flour is then emptied into the mixture and kneaded for five or ten minutes until the dough is firm and does not stick to your hands. After this the dough is cut into four sections, put into warmed, greased bread tins and left to rise in a warm place until the dough has doubled in size. Finally the tins are put in a very hot oven for about three-quarters of an hour; and after they are baked let them cool before putting them into the deep freeze.

Yet it is necessary to admit that the deep freeze, convenient though it may be, demands a great deal of Jeannie. It stands white and gleaming, an orange light at floor level denoting the motor is operating, constantly reminding her of the uses to which it can be put. Hence there are times when she appears to be the servant of the deep freeze rather than the other way round.

'I must spend the morning,' I will hear her say, 'making steak and kidney pies. We have only one left.'

Or:

'It's bread day tomorrow.'

Or:

'I have a whole basket of tomatoes which I must make into purée.'

103

The tomato purée is a basic content of the deep freeze; and there is the added appeal that we are no longer wasting the tomatoes which for one reason and another are not suitable for market, over-ripe tomatoes or misshapen. These we used to dump in a pile near the compost heap, giving delight to the blackbirds who considered them a delicacy, but causing distress to ourselves. The tomato purée, therefore, stored in one pint containers, has solved this problem of waste. There it is waiting, from one tomato season to another, to enrich a Provençale Bourguignonne or a Bolognaise sauce, or any other meat recipe which is enhanced by it.

Tomato purée, in any case, has a significance for me. This remark is not as absurd as it seems. Its significance is due to a freak period of my life when I founded a 'carry home a cooked meal' restaurant at Kingston-on-Thames, soon after the end of the war, one of the first of its kind.

The idea behind it seemed a good one. Food rationing was still stringent. Restaurant menus were limited and monotonous. Entertaining was very difficult; and I thought I had hit on an idea which would bring me a fortune. I foresaw a string of such restaurants. I imagined myself touring the sites and collecting the takings; and when, after a period, the success of the venture had become renowned, I would sell.

'Foolish,' a Savoy director warned Jeannie when she told him of the plans, 'your husband is very foolish.'

She repeated the comment to me, and I of course disregarded it. Business history is, after all, littered with Jonah-like warnings which have been proved false by those with initiative. Anyhow I was carried away by the enthusiasm which is my nature. I see no fun in life being told I am wrong even before I have made the effort to be right. Thus I launched the first restaurant, christened it The Larder, and looked forward to the bonanza.

It is soothing to look back upon a dismal period of one's life, and be able to say that at least one learnt something useful from it. It is a consolation prize for a time one otherwise wishes to forget. The consolation prize I had from The Larder was in the persons of two chefs, Bunny Pessione and Adam Almeida. Pessione was rotund, short and dark with black hair though in his late sixties; and an air about

104

him of a man who had failed to fulfill his ambitions. Almeida was shorter, always clasping his stomach as if in pain, always talking about his retirement one day to his native Portugal, always with smudges of flour on his face. Both were artists in their way. Both belonged to the pre-war age. Both possessed a sense of service which would now be considered archaic. Both were wasted at The Larder. Both joined with me at riling at some of the customers.

I quickly discovered that my image of myself as an observer-manager, rather than a direct participant, was a silly dream. This was very annoying. I was involved in other, far more important tasks, and I considered that the sort of things I ought to do in helping The Larder were the sort of things I least wanted to do. Yet I realised that the money I had invested, and the little I had to keep the business running, would soon disappear unless I undertook a personal interest in its every day affairs. For one thing Pessione and Almeida would lose heart; and for another it was impossible to expect any manageress both to deal with the customers over the counter and also cope with the stores which the chefs required for their kitchen.

Thus I found myself embroiled in a kind of life which I quickly detested. Loyal people were doing all they could to help my idea to become a success, yet I sensed it was already a failure. Money was running out. Dreams of my becoming a temporary tycoon and gaining the capital which would have given us independence ... these dreams were quickly disappearing. I was now working to save what I could of my investment. I had to face the fact that the only thing I could do was to cut my losses, and pray for a buyer to come along and save me from greater trouble.

But waiting for a buyer in any circumstances is an unnerving experience. You dare not leave the house, you rush to the telephone only to find the caller has the wrong number, and you spend hours of your time determining in your mind whether the couple who appeared so keen would ever come back with a firm offer. If, however, you are trying to sell a failing business, the experience is still more unnerving. You greet the first prospective buyer with a forced jauntiness as you are aware the asking price is far above the true value of the business. You greet another prospective buyer, then another, and another, though there are often intervals when no one shows any interest at all, until at last you would be happy to give the place away so as to relieve you of the strain. That's what I practically did with The Larder.

Meanwhile, as I waited, the two chefs gave me their support. Almeida would clutch a rolling pin, wave it in the air, crying: 'Fools, what fools! All this good food, and the damned public pass us by!'

I remember my increasing irritation with the public during this nerve-wracking time. I had dispensed with the manageress and had taken her place behind the counter. I was now in the front line. I had to keep calm as a customer stared at a hamburger, then asked if I would sell half of it. I had to put up with sadistic customers who complained that our delicious chicken *vol au vent* had no flavour. I had to cope with the superior tone of a lady, holding a white pekingese on a lead who after buying one of our special Cornish pasties, remarked: '*If* I like it, you will see me again.' We didn't.

I had to offer fake laughs to customers who made jokes. One looked at my new sports jacket, made a wry smile, and said: 'Hardly the right coat to wear here!' 'Why?' I asked. 'It looks horsey,' came the hearty reply. I had to try to be pleasant when a fat lady, overdressed, over bejewelled, demanded: 'One sausage roll, please.' 'Sorry, madam,' came my answer, 'there are no sausage rolls today.' 'What else is there then . . .?' A pause, then she added: 'There is nothing!' Yet there were ten dishes on the menu.

Then there were the obsequious remarks I found myself making: 'And what can I tempt you with today, madam?' Or: 'Change in the weather, madam . . . well, we mustn't grumble after a wonderful summer.' (This was repeated *ad nauseam*.) There were comments from customers, some of them bewildered. 'Can you tell us where to sit down?' Or: 'What a marvellous idea!' Or: 'It smells like heaven in here!' Or there was the old journalist who ruminated: 'Kingston is a town of visitors. After half past five in the evening the town shuts down and divides itself into four parishes . . . St Luke's, St Mark's, St John's, and All Saints. They are like four pieces of cheese in silver packets. They look very nice together in a box, but they do not belong to each other. And that is Kingston.'

106

The kitchens were within easy sight of the customers. That was one of the best ideas of The Larder. Everybody could see what was happening. Everybody could see where the dishes they were taking home had been prepared. They could see the chefs, and the chefs could see them, and listen.

Thus Pessione would hear me say to a customer who had bought fried fish: 'Would you like a portion of Sauce Tartare to go with it? The sauce is specially made by the chef.' And Passione would hear the reply. 'Heavens, no. I don't like those made up sauces, nor does my husband. We prefer our sauces out of a bottle.'

Pessione, for the most part, appeared to be a phlegmatic person, keeping his temperament under control; but there were occasions, and this was such an occasion, when he rivalled in temperament a great French chef called Vatel under whom he had worked before the First World War at the old Carlton in the Haymarket. Vatel was preparing a banquet for a company of notables; and when the fish from the fishmonger failed to arrive in time, he became so upset that he stabbed himself to death in a corner of the kitchens. Pessione used to tell this story as proof that great chefs were also great artists with passionate souls. He loved this story. He would tell it often; and I am sure that while at The Larder he imagined himself sometimes emulating his hero. But for a different reason.

'Sauce Tartare!' I heard him cry out after the customer had disappeared into the street, 'so she prefers a sauce out of a bottle to my Sauce Tartare!' I now saw he was brandishing a carving knife in the air. 'Criminal! Typical of the people today. Sauces out of bottles and mackintoshes. That's all they think of!' He was not, as it happens, referring to Mr Wilson. Mr Wilson was unknown at the time. 'Yes,' Pessione went on, his voice rising, Almeida with flour on his nose watching him, smiling, 'the days of great chefs are over. Nobody has standards any more. Me? I am lucky. I am finished' . . . then turning to me, 'Ah, Mr Tangye, I am sorry. These customers with their dull minds drive me crazy. You want your lunch? I will give you again Spaghetti Bolognaise. My speciality. You will enjoy it but . . .' and he grinned at me, 'the base of the sauce will have to come out of a bottle!' I well remember that bottle, and the others like it. A concentrate of tomato purée which Pessione despised;

but we could not possibly afford to make purée from fresh tomatoes, and I am sure the customers would not have known the difference in any case. Pessione, therefore, would have appreciated Jeannie s purée, 'Ah,' I can hear him saying, no longer brandishing a carving knife, 'here is something good. Here is an ingredient which would have pleased the great chefs of the past!'

The deep freeze was at its most demanding during the late summer. Always, of course, during the winter there had to be the bread days, the stew and goulash days, the steak and kidney days; but it was in late summer that the basic stores were laid down for the imaginary siege we were pretending to withstand.

Vegetables, for instance. I had already in the spring perused my Suttons catalogue, and consulted our old friend Percy Potter, who has a parson as a son, and who himself is in charge of the Sutton Trial Grounds at Gulval on the Hayle side of Penzance. We have known Percy, who later this winter was to help us plan next year's cottage garden, since we first came to Minack; and whenever we were in particular distress, when gales or frost or gluts had hit us badly, we used to go to Percy for comfort. He is an instinctive gardener. Though able to talk detachedly about his work, he was so at one with the mystical side of growing, the growing which has nothing to do with laboratory-inspired theory, that you felt while listening to him that you were in the company of a missionary. Growing, you realised, can never be a wholly scientific exercise. Growing will always require the instinct of a Percy Potter if a garden is to flourish.

We had, of course, the usual array of lettuces, beetroots, parsley, chives, carrots, marrows, and so on during the summer; and for the winter we would be planting out brussels sprouts and cauliflower. Our quest, therefore, when we visited Percy, was to discover which varieties of peas, broad beans, and runner beans we should grow that were suitable for deep freezing; and the results were Enorma runner beans, Early Onward peas, Green Giant Longpod broad beans, and Gullivert petit pois. We grew seventy-foot rows of each of them, and wondered whether we had grown enough. Late summer showed that we had done so. More than enough.

For when we came to preparing them for the deep freeze, we were faced with a task we had not foreseen. We had baskets and baskets to shell or shred. We had them up on the bridge, and we sat there during the summer day, side by side like two old maids, gossiping, breaking off every now and then to greet a caller, picking up a pea pod, opening it, watching the peas shoot into the basin.

'It's almost full. I'll go and weigh them.'

'Not on your own,' I would protest. 'I'll help. You're not going to leave me alone with these baskets.'

The peas weighed, polythene packets of a pound each taken to the deep freeze, we would return to our work. A pea pod picked up, opened, thrown away into another basket. The routine became therapeutic. A warm day, a chaffinch cheeping, two gulls on the roof, Fred pawing at the gate, boats passing, Lama in her nest gently snoring . . . I found it a peaceful occupation shelling Early Onward peas.

The broad beans, too, were peaceful, even more peaceful because being larger they filled the basin quicker. We began to run into trouble, however, when we started on the runner beans because we had only one shredder and we argued as to who should use it. Runner beans have to be shredded first before they are put into the deep freeze; and we had searched Penzance for another shredder. No luck.

'You use it,' I would say to Jeannie, as if I was offering her out of good manners the first glass from a bottle of champagne, 'do use it. I can manage with a knife.'

'I wouldn't dream of doing so. I am perfectly happy as I am.'

Our polite conversation was clearly a little unreal. Our mundane task had affected us. We were like anyone who operates within a very small world. We were making private jokes. We found it mildly amusing to talk in stilted language.

The language, on the other hand, was not stilted when we came to the Gullivert petit pois. These have always been a special favourite of mine; and I remember answering an advertisement in a newspaper once which offered those special tins of Belgian petit pois at a considerable discount; and I remember my anger when, after sending the money, I did not receive the tins. These petit pois did not make me angry. They made me exhausted. The deep freeze was already stuffed with broad beans, runner beans, and conventional peas ... yet we were up on the bridge, side by side, trying to fill the basin with the miserable, tiny petit pois. Hour after hour we popped the little things into the basin while the basin showed little sign of filling. Hour after hour. And now, months after their pods tested our patience, I have become doubtful that we were wise to grow them in the first place. Those we have had from the deep freeze do not seem to have the magical flavour I had expected from those Belgian tins which never arrived.

They are there, though, in the deep freeze, along with the others. Not only the peas, and the broad beans and the runner beans. We have also the blackberries picked by ourselves and any friends we could persuade to help us; and we have apple purée made from our own apples, and strawberries, and raspberries.

We have, therefore, the supplies with which to withstand our imaginary siege. We are independent.

And that, after all, is what we have sought since we came to Minack.

Yet how permanent can be independence?

CHAPTER TEN

Nellie had her independence.

When the rains came day after day, when the cold winds blew, when snipe rose, zigzagging in front of us as we walked up the lane to fetch our milk from Walter and Jack's farm at the top, when owls in the wood hooted messages on frosty nights, when fluttering flocks of linnets, finches and starlings raided a field then another, when summer snails were asleep in crevices, when the donkeys preferred to shelter in the stables, and we ourselves were glad to be indoors beside the fire, Nellie behaved as if she was impervious to the weather.

She continued to settle on the glass roof of the porch from time to time during the day; and when we threw grain to her on the ground, she was as bossy as ever towards the blue tits who tried to have a share. She was vociferous towards them. She burbled insults and threats, then she would make a dash at one who was proving to be too bold; and when the grain had gone, she would follow us as we walked by, expecting more. She was attached to us, that was clear. She liked our companionship, liked to observe the comings and goings of Minack, liked the way we took care of her; but she remained aloof. She had no intention of becoming a pet bird. We were a convenience, no more. She had no wish for us to touch her; and she was expert in evading our attempts to do so. And even in the stormiest weather, she always flew away at dusk.

'We must find out where she goes,' I said to Jeannie. I often said this.

I would say it at some point during the day with the intention that in the late afternoon I would put myself on sentry duty; and watch.

'If we went to Carn Barges,' I would add, 'and took our field-glasses, we could see her leave and the direction she takes.'

It seemed so easy. I had the time.

'Yes,' Jeannie would answer, 'let's do that.'

It was surprising, therefore, how the days and weeks

went by without putting our good intentions into practice. Something trivial was always enough to stop us. Brussels sprouts had to be picked for dinner, or the donkeys required attention, or I had to fetch coal or logs, or Lama wanted to have a stroll up the lane, expecting me to go with her. Then by the time these small tasks had been completed, I would find that Nellie had already gone. Or, if I was near her, I would hear the warning she always gave when she was about to go. She would coo a determined kind of coo, reminding me of a roll of drums heralding a great event.

Our behaviour on these winter evenings, this lack of will-power to follow up our wish to discover where Nellie flew away to, is evidence of the pleasant form of corruption which had engulfed us. We knew we had the time to amble through the day, and we were allowing ourselves to do so. The daffodil spikes were only beginning to show in rows, and blooms could not be expected until the middle of January; and I was not writing a book. This was the between times of the year, between summer and spring harvests, and we were at liberty to do what we liked with our time. Thus we found ourselves putting off making decisions, however small. We relaxed; and enjoyed this particular form of corruption.

Yet there were moments when we had a sense of guilt that we were content. After all it is unfashionable to be content. It is an age of protest, and of injustice real or imaginary, and of violence, and of haste, and of the cynic who knocks the pleasant aspects of life. Any good cause, or person of integrity, is a potential victim of the cynic. It is so easy to win sniggering laughs by knocking. I listened not long ago to one of the professional cynics making witty comments about King George VI. The King, he inferred, had been a nonentity, a colourless figurehead, someone whom the present generation should laugh at. But those of us who lived through his times, through the war period when surrender would have been inevitable unless there had been a man like the King upon whom to focus our loyalty, will always remember him with great admiration. And I will also always remember a sentence from the speech he made on V.E. Day.

'Let none of us,' said the King, 'do anything unworthy of what those who have died would have expected of us, or let our children ever do anything unworthy of what was sacrificed for them.'

But Jeannie and I did not allow our fleeting moments of guilt to interfere with the enjoyment of each day. We were now experiencing the kind of life we had always wanted to experience. We were not rushed. We had no need to see people. We had comforts around us. We had worked hard, and thus this idleness was a holiday. We were aware of our luck, and neither of us took it for granted.

'What shall we do today?' I would say to Jeannie as I lit my pipe after breakfast. I smoke a mixture called Down the Road which comes from the old family firm of Simmons in Burlington Arcade. I have smoked the same mixture for years; and soon after I met Jeannie we were walking together down the Arcade and I pointed out the shop to her. 'That's my tobacco shop,' I said, 'and where I get my pipes.' She said afterwards that she thought I was giving her a hint. She insists that I also added: 'Every girl should know the whereabouts of her man friend's tobacco shop.' I am sure she is imagining this. I have to admit, though, that she gave me a pipe soon after that walk down the Arcade.

'What shall we do?'

First there were the mundane tasks which had to be done, like tidying the cottage and washing up. We do not have anyone to help inside the cottage; and though there would be obvious advantages if there was such a person, we both relish the freedom we have as a result of being on our own. We do not have to do any cajoling, or wondering why extra presents are not appreciated, or any soothing of mysterious, ruffled tempers. True we have been lucky in those who have helped in the past but we prefer to be free. And on those occasions when Jeannie momentarily regrets the tasks she has to do, I pick up a Bristol glass hand-bell which I bought long ago, and which is known by us as the Freedom Bell. I pick it up and ring it.

'We ought to move the wine,' said Jeannie

'That won't take long.'

'We've been meaning to move it for ages.'

'All right,' I said, with sudden decisiveness, 'before I do anything else I'll carry the cases to the donkey house.'

The donkey house was another name for the stables where the donkeys had the opportunity to spend the rough

113

winter nights; and because the walls were arm-length thick, it was a warm place to be; and suitable for the storage of the wine Jeannie had made. The cases were of cardboard.

'Only hope,' I added, 'that the donkeys won't eat the cardboard.'

'If they do,' said Jeannie, 'they are unlikely to pull out the corks.'

'But supposing they suddenly lash out and kick the bottles and break them?'

'Isn't this where it all began,' asked Jeannie mildly, 'isn't this why we haven't moved the cases? . . . all because we waste our time wondering what the donkeys might do?'

I laughed.

'Agreed.'

We used to despise home-made wine. We used to consider it a concoction devised by worthy people who needed a hobby. Then a couple of years ago we experimented, produced a few bottles of elderberry champagne and elderberry claret, and found them delicious. Then we looked at our wine bills, and asked ourselves why we were wasting money. We had the opportunity on our doorstep to make all the *vin ordinaire* we needed; and we calculated, without allowing for the labour involved, that it would cost little more than five new pence a bottle.

We are now aware, of course, that home wine-making is rapidly becoming a profession, and not just a hobby. The economical reasons for this are obvious; and those who take their wine-making seriously can organise a cellar of very high quality. I am not, of course, referring to instant wine made out of packets which you can buy at a chemist. The old recipes are the ones to follow, the same that have been used by countrymen for generations; and based on ingredients which abound in the countryside.

In due course Jeannie and I intend to experiment still further. We have a list of old recipes given to Jeannie by her aunt who is an expert; and they include wines from marigolds, primroses, cowslips, rose petals, clover, dandelions and hawthorn blossom. Then you can make wine from beetroots, carrots, celery, pea pods, and old potatoes. Potato wine, we are assured, tastes like dry sherry after letting it stand for three months, and like old brandy if left for over a year. Gorse petal wine is another good one; and so is blackberry which matures like a kind of *vin rosé*. I would not believe the claims made for any of these wines, were it not for the success we have had with our elderberries.

The elderberry champagne is made from the flowers of the elder-tree, picked during June; and the claret from the berries picked in September and October. The elder-tree itself plays a large part in folk lore, particularly in regard to its healing qualities. The flowers once upon a time were used as the base for a healing ointment for cuts and burns. The freshly gathered leaves, warmed in an oven, are supposed to relieve headaches when pressed against the head. The berries, when green and stewed in camphorated oil, become a medicine for coughs and bronchitis. Then there are the superstitions which haunt the tree. An unhappy home will become a happy one if a tree is coaxed to flourish in the garden; and such a tree will ward off wickedness, so that anyone advancing with evil thoughts on the house and its occupants finds himself powerless. Such a legendary background enhances the pleasure of drinking the wine. We are put in a virtuous mood. We are benefiting our bodies as well as stimulating our minds. No wonder we had made several cases both of the champagne and the claret which I now had to move to the donkey house.

The move was no distance. Our wine-making centre was in one half of the small greenhouse where we bunch daffodils in the spring, and weigh tomatoes in the summer. It was a convenient place for the equipment because there was a bench for the jars and buckets, and a cement floor where the messy side of wine-making could be done. It need not, however, be all that messy. It is just a question of trying to avoid spilling the contents of the bucket when transferring these contents to the jars; and of trying to avoid spilling the contents of the jars when transferring them to the bottles. Having said this, let me explain how we achieved this cellar of wines from which we will be drinking next summer.

We picked the elder flowers on sunny days when they were scenting, and when they were fully opened and the petals were beginning to fall. We picked them from the many elders we have at Minack, some bordering the lane, some down the cliff where they act as hedges around the daffodil meadows. In summer, of course, the daffodil leaves have

115

died back and the meadows are covered by lush grass and vegetation; and this gives pleasure and feed for the donkeys. The donkeys usually accompanied us on these expeditions, and they would watch puzzled as I climbed up to a branch to collect a handful of flowers. Is he doing it for us? He's filling that yellow bucket, let's put our noses into it. They would then advance on me, and I had to push them away, thinking nevertheless that it was pleasant to be accompanied by donkeys in one's own vineyard so close to the sea.

We had to measure the quantity of the flowers, and we did this by gently pressing the flowers into a quart jug until it was full. This we did when we returned to the greenhouse, putting them back afterwards into the plastic bucket. Then, for each quart jug of flowers, we brought a gallon of water to the boil in a preserving pan containing a pound of seedless raisins and two and a half pounds of preserving sugar, letting it simmer for half an hour and removing the scum. We next poured this through a sieve over the flowers in the bucket; and when it had cooled, we added the strained juice of a lemon and an ounce of dried yeast scattered on the surface. We then left this to brew for a fortnight, stirring each day with a wooden spoon (never a metal one); and then strained all the contents though a piece of butter muslin and a funnel into a gallon glass jar. The jar has a special stopper which enables the brew to ferment without bursting the jar; and there followed the pleasantest part of wine-making. We were able to watch the brew at work, bubbling, until several weeks later when there was no more bubbling to be seen and the wine was ready to go into bottles.

The method of making claret was similar. We picked the berries, shredding them from the stalks, then went through the same routine as for the champagne except we used demerara sugar instead of preserving sugar and did not add raisins. As for the pleasure the wine will give, I can only say that last year's vintage was magnificent. The champagne had a soft effervescence, and a flavour like the true scent of elderberry flowers on sunny days; and the claret had a body to it, and a style, that deceived a guest, an expert on wine, into asking who shipped the claret. Unfortunately, although we had this summer many more bottles than we had for the first year of experiment, there was still not enough. They had all gone by the time I was moving the cases of the new vintage; and we now have to wait till next summer before we taste this new vintage. Jeannie believes it will be finer than ever before.

My grandfather, Sir Richard Tangye, disapproved of alcohol in any form; beer, spirits or wine. He claimed that his total abstinence was a basic reason for his successful life, and he never ceased telling his friends, work associates, and his children to follow his example. The children were loth to do so. My aunt Elsie told me that she so rebelled against his fanatical attitude that she used to slip into the bar of Snow Hill station in Birmingham, and have a quick one; and she gulped the drink as a gesture of defiance. Nor was my father teetotal, though he believed that neither myself nor my two brothers should drink alchohol before we were twenty-one. He therefore offered us each £100 if we did not do so, and put us on our honour to keep our side of the bargain. My two elder brothers collected their money but I, alas, was out of luck. At the age of twenty my father, one of the most generous men I have ever known, explained to me that his funds were low, that he would not be able to give the £100, and so I could do what I liked. Even then I never went into a pub until I was nearly twenty-two, but that perhaps was for a snobbish reason. My Harrovian education had led me to believe that pubs were vulgar, and not the happy, friendly places I later found them to be.

My grandfather was a remarkable man. He was born at Illogan near Redruth, one of five brothers. His own grandfather came from St Columb near Newquay where he worked as a boy on a farm. He was still a boy when he decided to set out for the tin mines of west Cornwall, and he walked on his own, except for his small dog, all the way to Illogan carrying on his back his only possession, a saddle. There he obtained a night job in the mines, and shortly after some rough land of rocks and gorse, and this he worked at during the day. He lived to his nineties, and Richard describes in one of his books how the old man died. A Citizen Kane kind of end . . . for he relived that walk from St Columb to Illogan and his last words were: 'Has the little dog come in yet?' Richard himself a dog lover delighted in this sentimental story. He also described it as a lesson in loyalty.

117

His father had a shop in Broad Lane, Illogan, and also ten acres of land which he used to plough in Quaker dress and broad-brimmed hat. The sons, however, had no intention of following this quiet profession; and in any case four of them had the qualities of genius. Richard and George were the ones with a business flair; Joseph and James, particularly James, were the inventors. So in due course these four left Illogan to find fortune in the Midlands and within twenty years they had founded the Cornwall Works in Birmingham where two thousand people were to be employed, and had also made the name of Tangye world famous for its engineering products.

Often their inventions came before their time. A bicycle proved a failure because it seemed to be so unusual; and the 'road locomotive' was a failure because the landed gentry were afraid that their horses would take flight at the sight and the sound of it. But the road locomotive was a remarkable achievement. The Tangye brothers called it the Cornubia; and it could travel at twenty miles an hour, and could carry ten people. The first Cornubia was on the road in the early 1860's and created enormous public interest; and the brothers were right to believe they were about to make their fortune. But the landed gentry had powerful friends in Parliament; and as a consequence an Act was passed forbidding any machine to proceed along the highway at more than four miles an hour, and even then it had to have a man walking in front holding a red flag. This did not deter the Tangye brothers. They scrapped the Cornubia, and set about developing other inventions.

They had already had one major success; and this was an improved version of the hydraulic jack which on a day in January 1858 was to create a legend. Isambard Brunel had built his steamship the *Great Eastern*, and found he was unable to launch his ship down the slipway into the Thames. The jacks he was using would not budge her. Having heard of the Tangye invention, he told his agent to contact the brothers. They still at that time had only a small workshop in Birmingham which was down an entry behind a baker's shop (the baker's oven saved the expense of heating the workshop); and when the agent one dark evening rang the bell, he was sure he had come to the wrong place. He apologised for his mistake when Richard opened the door. 'I'm looking for Tangye's,' the man explained, 'Mr Brunel needs their jacks to launch the *Great Eastern*!' Forever afterwards Richard used to say: 'We launched the *Great Eastern*, and the *Great Eastern* launched us.' Twenty years later Tangye jacks gained further fame when they hoisted Cleopatra's Needle into position on the Victoria Embankment; and one of the jacks was placed in a recess of the base where it still lies, along with worthy companions including a map of the London of the time, the book of Genesis in Arabic and Hebrew, copies of the newspaper of the day, weights and measures, and copies of the Bible in various languages. I have often walked along the Embankment, or looked down upon the obelisk from one of the Savoy windows, and felt proud that my family played a leading part in placing it there.

Richard, apart from his business acumen, was a man of liberal ideas. He was a great philanthropist, kept to strict rules of honour throughout his life, believed his work people were as good as himself and that they should always receive a fair reward for their work. He expected their loyalty as a result (there were never any strikes at the Cornwall Works), and was convinced that a job of a great industrialist was to be paternal. His paternalism certainly produced reforms. He was the first industrialist in this country to introduce the nine-hour day, the first to give a half-day on Saturday, the first to pay wages on a Friday, the first to provide a canteen for the workers, and the first to provide a free health service. These reforms were strongly supported by all the brothers, especially George, but they caused displeasure among other industrialists; for the reforms were taking place towards the end of the nineteenth century, and the industrial barons resented the Tangye brothers weakening their power by a liberal example.

Richard, in fact, could have become a politician of note. He was repeatedly asked to stand for Parliament and Gladstone urged him to stand for Birmingham. Lord Rosebery, too, was anxious that he should enter political life. But my grandfather seemed to consider a political career of little appeal because he believed a successful industrialist could serve the community more usefully by retaining his freedom. Nor did he believe in honours. A peerage did not interest him, and he only in the end accepted his knighthood because he truly considered it as a compliment to the people of the Cornwall Works.

He was also a collector, and a great traveller. He was a frail man, small with a flowing beard, and I marvel at his energy and his boldness in carrying out his travels. America, Australia, New Zealand ... he made journeys to such places in little boats, unperturbed by the discomfort. He and his brother George gathered together the finest private collection of Wedgwood pottery in the world, then presented it to the City of Birmingham (a few pieces were kept in the family and Jeannie has a brooch from a medallion); and he also became one of the great authorities on Cromwell, writing a notable book called *The Two Protectors—Oliver and Richard Cromwell*.

My mother, however, did not like him. 'A funny little man,' she used to say, dismissing him in a feminine way; and I have often wondered why. My mother was a darling person who devoted herself completely to the bringing up of us three boys. She was prepared happily to make any sacrifice if it had the likelihood of advancing the happiness of myself or that of my two brothers; and I have never had any doubt that she possessed a selfless and generous nature. Yet she disliked my grandfather; or perhaps she was frightened of him. I think also it is likely that she failed to impose her personality upon my grandfather; and this nettled her. At the time she married Gilbert my father, Richard was a dying man; and I can understand that he might have been suspicious of my mother's flirtatious ways. She intended by her manners to show him the warmth she had for the Tangye family; but he, I guess, interpreted her youthful enthusiasm as being an affront to his Cromwellian principles. In any case, my mother's rebuff, if she did indeed receive a deliberate rebuff, resulted in my never realising my grandfather's true worth until years after I should have done.

I wonder, too, why my father did not enlighten me. My father was a successful barrister before the 1914 war when he volunteered and entered Intelligence. After it was over he decided to stay in the army instead of returning to the law; and I believe it was a decision he always regretted. There were, however, compensations, not the least being able to satisfy his love of music. The England of that time had a philistine attitude towards music while in Germany, in Cologne and Wiesbaden where we lived, the opera houses were playing to enraptured audiences; and legendary singers were appearing like Lotte Lehmann and Frederick Schorr, and conductors such as Bruno Walter and Otto Klemperer. Such performers provided emotional experiences for myself and my brothers; and my father helped us in every way to indulge in them. In my holidays from my English preparatory school, I would spend three or four nights a week at the opera house and, because evening dress was obligatory, I would wear an Eton collar, the uncomfortable starched Eton collar, as I sat through four hours of *The Mastersingers*. My taste was catholic. I loved Puccini, and was undaunted by *The Ring*, was thrilled equally by Richard and Johann Strauss, delighted in Mozart, and was specially excited when on an advance poster I saw that an obscure opera like *Die Toten Augen* by d'Albert was to be performed. I am in everlasting debt to my father that he awoke me to music; and now, years later, as I sit sometimes in the cottage at Minack, listening for a whole evening, for instance, to *Karajan* and the *Gotterdamerung*, and at moments becoming as emotional as I became when I first listened to the music as a small boy, I return in my mind to my seat in the dress circle of the Cologne opera house, and I am wearing again my Eton collar.

When my father returned from Germany, he soon became Joint Chairman of the Cornwall Quarter Sessions, and then, until he died during the Second World War he performed, endlessly, various public duties. He was also for a period, chairman of Tangyes though it was now a very different business from that of my grandfather's day. The business was struggling to survive. For more than thirty years it never paid a dividend though the employees continued to be looked after in a benevolent manner. The origin of this debacle was due to praiseworthy high-mindedness during the First World War years, when engineering firms were making huge profits out of munitions and war materials. Tangyes, however, refused to make a penny profit; and when the war ended and the slump came, they did not have the reserves to cope with the situation. There is no Tangye in the firm now and it belongs to a combine.

Glendorgal was my father's home as it had been Richard's.

121

It had a glorious position above its own inlet of a bay at Porth near Newquay; and it faced up the north coast, the high jagged coastline of Watergate Bay, Bedruthan Steps and in the far distance Trevose Head. It was here that my grandfather kept his unique collection of Cromwellian relics which later became part of the Wallace Collection in Stafford Place after the Tangye family had given it to the nation. It was housed at Glendorgal in a large room with a glass roof, and which I knew as the billiard-room when I was a boy. I used to play billiards by the hour either by myself or with my father; and occasionally with my brothers. My brothers, then, were remote people to me; and years later they told me that they didn't even notice my existence until I went to Harrow. We had left Germany by then. Later on, when we began bringing girls to Glendorgal, the billiard-room became a party room; and after dinner we would adjourn with our girls to the party room while our parents sedately read their papers. We used to listen to the *Welte*, a superior kind of pianola or automatic piano, which my father had brought back from Germany, or to a record player, or to the piano itself being played by one of ourselves. We used to sit in an alcove of the billiard-room on a long curved seat covered by worn leather, with the huge window behind us facing up the north coast I have described; and at night, when we looked through it, we could watch the winking of Trevose lighthouse just as today I can watch from Minack the winking of the Lizard light. My father, for some reason, always called the Trevose light Becky's Eye. The girls we brought to Glendorgal lived in London, for we knew no local girls. The girls were young actresses, and models, and some who had nothing else to do except to be debs; and we used to bring them for long weekends, hastening to and from Cornwall in our cars. I wonder what has happened to some of them, what they did with their lives. When we sat in that alcove we believed life stretched without end in front of us, only momentary problems to solve, like the young in any age, the same outlook except for the fashions of the time. But within a year or two these pretty things were in uniform, or in love with a pilot in the Battle of Britain, or driving ambulances as the bombs fell on London.

I loved Glendorgal in the same way I now love Minack. I belonged. I knew every part of it, every incline, every rock;

and I was emotionally involved in the place so that there was hardly a corner of it which did not share with me some secret, personal experience. When I went to Glendorgal I never wanted to leave its environment, just as now I never want to leave Minack. Both belong in my mind to a world which is untamed; and therefore true and unselfconscious. I never knew an unhappy moment at Glendorgal.

My father was an example to me for the love of roots. His public duties took him often away from his home but, whereas others would have stretched a visit to three days, my father would hurry back to Glendorgal within two. He loved my mother. That was one reason; and in forty odd years of their marriage there was not a day, even during the wars, that he did not write to her if they had not seen each other; and yet Glendorgal was in a way even more important to him than my mother. Glendorgal gave him a mystical sense of security. He was, like all the Cornish, inspired in the final instance by Cornish magic. The Cornish, and this is their secret, are aware that the senses provide happiness. Materialism doesn't, except that it helps. Only a fool would say it doesn't help.

My father, therefore, awakened in me the emotional side of living yet, erudite man though he was, failed to educate me. I do not remember him ever extolling the virtues of 'the little man' who was his father. Probably this was my fault. He may have tried, and I had shown no interest. I have often been amazed in retrospect at the periods in my life when I have been blind to the advantages which were staring me in the face. If someone is prepared to unfold his experience and knowledge, the listener must be in the mood to be receptive; and there have been many times in my life when I was not in the mood. Thus I do not blame my father for my failure to benefit from what he could have offered me. I am thankful enough that I inherited from him his love of Cornwall.

Snow fell before Christmas, and Nellie continued to fly away from Minack at dusk. Geoffrey had made a loft for her out of an old box and fixed it high up on the wall in the barn, a cosy home in such weather, but though she would sit there during the day, she did not like it as a bedroom. She had a better place to go. Where?

We do not often have snow. Once, in our time here, there was a day-long blizzard which blocked our road into St

123

Buryan, and it remained blocked for a week; and there was a legendary blizzard at the end of the last century which isolated many of the farms for six weeks. On the present occasion the snow was thick enough in the lane to prevent a car driving up the hill; and so I was glad that I had taken heed of the snow warnings and taken the car up to the top by the farm buildings, and left it there. When the snow ceased falling, the wind had gone round to the east, and it was bitter cold.

We do not mind snow, now that we do not grow crops, like violets, which can be hurt by it; and we even like it because there is amusement in tracing the spoors . . . the V sign of rabbits, the straight line of a fox, the spread of a badger, the petals of a cat. A simple pleasure, but sometimes illuminating; and we were following at dusk the fresh spoor of a fox, along the path towards the onion meadow and the Pentewan meadows, and we had reached the boundary which divides them when a pigeon skimmed our heads. It had disappeared within a second into the cold greyness, but not before we saw the direction it was taking.

We had found at last the whereabouts of Nellie's sleeping quarters.

CHAPTER ELEVEN

Nellie's sleeping quarters, we now realised, were close to the lighthouse. Nobody lives at the lighthouse. It is half a mile away on the Pentewan cliff, and is hidden from our sight by the hill behind us. Nor do we see it from any other part of our land, save from a couple of meadows that lie below the onion meadow. Strange, however, for Nellie to choose such a place. There was a flashing light that might have been expected to disturb her, and the sound of the fog signal known as Howard's Howl.

Some people consider Howard's Howl a romantic sound, a reminder of the wildness of this coast, conjuring up a picture of small boats fighting great seas. One person thought it a reassuring sound. 'Isn't it company for you in that lonely place of yours?' he asked.

Such cosy impressions however, are not shared by Jeannie and me. We know too much about Howard's Howl. We have heard it too often howling away when the visibility around us is clear. On such occasions I sometimes jump in the car and drive to the nearest telephone box and telephone the duty officer of the Trinity headquarters in Penzance.

'You can see right across the bay,' I will say in desperation, 'can't you turn the damn thing off?'

He can't. He has to obey the Trinity House regulations; and these regulations decree that if there is less than three miles visibility at Tol Pedn coastguard station five miles up the coast from the lighthouse, the fog signal must be switched on; and also the same situation exists at Penzance five miles down the coast; and most curious of all, if there is fog thirty miles away across the bay at the lighthouse on the Lizard.

Thus, although our lighthouse is described as automatic by Trinity House, it is only automatic as far as the light is concerned. This turns on as soon as dusk falls, but Howard's Howl? A report comes in from Tol Pedn or the Lizard, and the controller at Penzance presses the button. Five miles away we hear the result.

'Blast it!' I cry, 'Howard's Howl is at it again, and I can count six ships on the distant horizon!'

The irritation we feel is, of course, insignificant compared with others who have noise problems. We have no whine of aircraft to disturb our days and nights. We have no drills roaring on a building site. We have no traffic to shatter us into taking its thunder for granted. We are lucky therefore. We are only irritated.

We are particularly irritated because Howard's Howl is an unreliable warning system. Its effectiveness depends upon which way the wind is blowing. We can tell, because when the wind is blowing up the coast away from us, we can scarcely hear Howard's Howl. But if the wind is blowing from the south towards us, the sound can be heard on the road halfway to Penzance; and if this is at night, sleeping countrymen are awakened by the sound far inland.

Thus Howard's Howl is of dubious value, for if it is a rough sea, a strong wind blowing, only boats sailing against the wind will hear it. There is a good reason, therefore, why some people argue that its cost could have been better spent elsewhere . . . helping to eliminate black spots on the road for instance. Motorists are far more in need of help than some occasional sailor who has carelessly strayed off course.

Weeks go by, however, when the weather is clear all round the coast, and Howard's Howl is silent, and we find ourselves forgetting that its electronic note exists. This was the case this Christmas. All through December it had kept quiet, and neither ourselves nor Nellie had been disturbed. Not that we knew until now that Nellie was sleeping her nights so close to it.

'Let's find out this evening,' I said to Jeannie next day, 'exactly where she's going to. If we're by the lighthouse steps a quarter of an hour before dusk we'll be able to see her flying in from Minack.'

It is one of the luxuries of having time to spare that we could indulge in such a frivolous quest. These minor moments of pleasure are repeated all through the year, pointless moments perhaps, but helping to provide a depth to living.

'It's time,' Jeannie replied, 'that we did so. Silly Nellie, flying away from the comfort we offer her.'

We were, I suppose, a little put out by her behaviour. Geoffrey had made her a splendid box in which she could shel-

126

ter from the weather, and yet she ignored it. She preferred to desert us at the very moment when the temperature was swiftly dropping, flying away from the comfort of Minack, in favour of some ledge on a cliff.

It was bitterly cold when we set off. It had been bitterly cold all day; and the water-butt by the corner of the cottage had remained frozen over; so, too, the donkeys' water trough, once the china kitchen sink, but now wedged in the hedge of the field above the cottage, a pipe connecting it with the tank by the well. The pipe was frozen also; and I reckoned we were lucky that the main pipe to the cottage was still running.

Blackbirds and redwings clucked their warning notes as we walked along the grass path towards the onion meadow and the Pentewan boundary. Redwings distress me. I have watched them in many winters when the cold comes, foraging in the banks after the sun of the morning has melted the snow and softened the earth; and there is always a mood of desperation about their efforts. They belong to the thrush family, and nest in the far north of Scandinavia so that you would have expected they were immune to cold. At the first sign of winter they fly across the North Sea in their thousands, settle in the north until Britain, too, begins its winter, then start to fly south. They now seem to panic. They fly south, south, south, just ahead of the frost and the snow, across Dorset, Somerset, Devon until they reach the north coast of Cornwall, then down the coast to Land's End, round the corner, and up again in their thousands, lemming like, along the cliffs of Mount's Bay, up the south coast into the very cold again. I have picked up dozens of casualties in some winters, some I have tried to save, taking them into the warmth, but I have never succeeded. They are easy victims of pneumonia, and no care can help them.

We reached the boundary between our land and the Pentewan meadows, climbed over the stone stile we have built there, went past the Trinity House notice declaring that no one was allowed in the vicinity of the lighthouse, then crossed the thirty lace meadow. A lace is the Cornish means of measuring a meadow. A lace is, in fact, six yards by six yards; and in our potato days we used to follow the custom of our neighbours by judging the extent of our crop by the quantity extracted from each lace. Hence if in some meadow we dug

127

half a hundredweight of potatoes per lace, it was a very bad crop. If it was two hundredweight, it was a very good one. The thirty lace meadow, however, when we worked the Pentewan meadows, unfailingly produced a bad crop. The potatoes were always the size of marbles.

We went on past the Dairyman's Meadow where seventy years ago a donkey used to graze. An elderly lady came to Minack the other day who lived as a child in the same Pentewan cottage where Jane used to live when she was working for us. She told us how her father used to use this donkey to carry the potatoes up from the lower meadows on the cliff; and how she herself, as a child, was taught to drive the donkey in a trap, driving it regularly into St Buryan. Naturally she asked if Penny and Fred did any work; and I replied that they didn't, only gave pleasure. I half expected her to snort a reply that I wasn't making proper use of them but to my surprise she said how wise I was to let them live their life in this way. 'Our donkey,' she explained, 'had the usual donkey fate of being asked to do more than he was capable of doing. One morning he was carrying up a load of potatoes from where the lighthouse now stands, and it was too heavy for him. Just as he reached the path that leads to the cottage, he slipped. And he broke his fetlock. Father killed him then, there was nothing else he could do . . . and he buried him in one of the meadows by the path.'

Just past the Dairyman's Meadow is a hut, known as the Pink Hut. It was a hut built of corrugated iron before the First World War, painted red, and now faded into a dirty pink. Here we used to 'shoot' our seed potatoes, remorselessly picking each one from the sack in which they had travelled from Scotland, and setting it side by side with the others, eyes of the potatoes facing upwards. It was here, too, that we helped save a badger caught in a gin trap, which had been released by the trapper who had taken pity on it. For weeks we fed it with bread and milk. And then one day we arrived at the Pink Hut, and found, it seemed, that a pick axe had been at work on the wood based floor. It was, however, only the badger. He had recovered. He was well enough to leave. He had dug his way to freedom.

We now reached the site of the lighthouse. There was an old quarry biting into the side of a hill above it, the stone of which, in the middle of the last century, built the lanes of St